THE WORD
AND THE WORDS

THE WORD
AND
THE WORDS

COLIN MORRIS

Nashville   ABINGDON PRESS   New York

THE WORD AND THE WORDS

Copyright © 1975 by Colin Morris

First published in U.S. by Abingdon Press and in Great Britain
by Epworth Press, 1975.

Library of Congress Cataloging in Publication Data

Morris, Colin M
  The Word and the words.
  1. Preaching   I. Title.

BV4211.2.M67   251   75-15955

ISBN 0-687-46045-X

MANUFACTURED BY THE PARTHENON PRESS AT
NASHVILLE, TENNESSEE, UNITED STATES OF AMERICA

This book is dedicated to my sisters

IRENE AND ELSIE

with love and gratitude

FOREWORD

———

Dr COLIN MORRIS sees preaching for what it is—an exciting and an awesome calling. That is abundantly clear in this book, and for that reason, among many others, I welcome its appearance and am privileged to be asked to write a Foreword.

The writer has been, and is, engaged in Christian action, political action, missionary action, the action of the mass media. But he believes that the most powerfully active force at work in God's world is the word of God operating in men and women obedient to that word. 'The articulation of God's imperious demand, the offer of his forgiveness and the gift of his grace'—this he sees to be at the heart of any preaching worthy of the name.

I wish this book a very wide circulation. It will give its readers many a chuckle; it will elicit from some of them a frown of dissent. So be it. But it cannot do other than convey to any reader who treats it with the intelligence that it deserves that preaching is an activity of immense moment, totally demanding on him who undertakes it, crucially important to him who hears it.

I pray that it will do much towards that re-instatement of the ministry of the word which is perhaps the modern Church's greatest need.

✠ DONALD CANTUAR

Lambeth Palace
1975

INTRODUCTION

LIKE the Lectures on which it is based, this book is a defence of classical preaching, by which I mean the proclamation of the Word through the sermon as it has been understood in Christian history. This deliberate narrowing of my terms of reference leaves me open to the charge that I have side-stepped a plethora of sociological and theological controversies, let alone linguistic ones. Indeed, the fundamental question whether the sermon as a form of communication has any validity in the modern world is left virtually unanswered, or at least, is answered in the affirmative because I believe in preaching in the traditional sense. In no way do I belittle other methods of communicating the Gospel, and I observe with admiration and not a little puzzlement some of the exciting experiments in ways of stating Christian truth through drama, dialogue, the dance and so on. But they are not for me; hence, I try to avoid that prevalent Christian error—attempting to do badly what others can do well to the neglect of things they are not doing at all.

Even the structure I have imposed on this book—the use, in the main, of paradoxical affirmations about the nature of preaching has, of necessity, limited my analysis. The ground I cover is restricted and there are some preachers who may well feel that certain themes are missing or given too scant treatment. This I readily acknowledge, but the book is based on a finite number of Lectures and though I had not exhausted my store of possible paradoxes, I frankly have not had time to take the book far beyond the scope of the draft from which I originally spoke.

Any preacher's approach to his task is obviously conditioned by his experience. In my own case, I occupied the same pulpit on Zambia's Copperbelt for thirteen years during the ferment and fury of the freedom struggle. This has given a bent to my preaching which has permanently shaped its style. Then three years at Wesley's Chapel in London, the Mother Church of World Methodism, the majority of whose congregation was made up of visitors from all over the globe worshipping there for the first and probably the only time. Neither of these preaching situations could possibly be called normal. I have never known the strengths and problems of Methodist circuit ministry; and suburbia, the inner city, rural areas and university chaplaincies are all foreign to my experience. I make this confession at the outset because the percipient reader will detect it anyway.

I have from time to time committed my sermons to print. This is, of course, a grave error from one angle. Try repeating a sermon after it has been published and any members of a congregation who may have read it feel they are being treated to warmed up left-overs. There is also the risk of having a sermon preached back at oneself. This is a salutary and sometimes harrowing experience. Not that the preacher is committing a heinous offence—for which sermon in the last resort is truly original?—but rather because a strange voice, a different context and the homiletical gem one has polished with *such* loving care as to be blind to its flaws, is revealed for the bauble it truly is. However, it is inevitable that a preacher should quote from his own works in a book on the sermon, if only to draw negative morals. I have used not only ideas but whole passages of *Mankind My Church*, published in 1971 by Hodder and Stoughton. I do so with the permission of Mr Edward England of that great publishing house, to whom I am indebted for his understanding and Christian courtesy.

On scanning the quotations from other authors, I am struck by the number which originate from Victorian and early twentieth-century works on preaching. It is a curious thing that if an author invokes the authority of Christian thinkers who lived centuries ago, for example Luther, Calvin or Wesley, it is accounted to him as scholarship if not righteousness. But great preachers of a couple of generations or so ago are reckoned to be 'dated'. They are just old enough to be unfashionable but too recent to be venerable. Yet books such as Phillips Brooks' *Lectures on Preaching*, J. H. Jowett's, *The Preacher—His Life and Work*, P. T. Forsyth's *Positive Preaching and the Modern Mind* and Paul Scherer's *For We Have This Treasure*—all four given as Lyman-Beecher Lectures on Preaching at Yale University— will retain their power and relevancy so long as a single preacher survives to mount the pulpit steps to announce the Good News of the Gospel. After all, the most important quotations in this book—from the New Testament—are almost two thousand years' old. And the preacher who doubts *their* topicality is in the wrong job.

Any preacher who presumes to give advice to his fellow practitioners tends to feel a little like a bald-headed man selling hair restorer. 'Who is *he* to tell *us*?' they not unnaturally ask. There is generally an embarrassing gap between one's profession and practice in any field of Christian endeavour, and it is only partially filled by George Bernard Shaw's often-quoted aphorism—Those who can, do; those who can't, teach. It particularly behoves the author of a book about preaching to approach both his subject and his readers in an attitude of humility. I blush when I recount my early attempts to put together something which bore a vague resemblance to a sermon. I knew all the answers and could summon a prodigious number of words in which to couch them. Congregations endured my cocksure verbosity with fortitude and to them I owe a deep debt of gratitude.

Because I do a modest amount of broadcasting and television, it may be wondered why I make no reference to these powerful media which bring millions within the range of one's voice. The short answer is that this is *not* a book on communication as such. That is a complex subject which I have not studied in any depth, possibly because I have been too busy communicating. For me, evangelism is a face-to-face encounter—a two-way process, or more strictly, three if the Holy Spirit is taken into account. Religious radio and television I regard as exercises in pre-evangelism whose aim is to pose a question in the listener or viewer's mind, challenge his values, explore his life-style. In other words, convert him from a spectator or eavesdropper into an honest inquirer. The TV screen in particular is much like a shop-window. The trick is to get the window-shopper through the front door of the store. Then it is up to the salesman to do the rest. I admit the crudity of such an analogy but trust the reader to accept its main point without assuming that it expresses in detail my basic approach to evangelism.

One or two points about style and content are in order. When I compare what I have written with the high tone of some of the classical works on preaching, I am conscious of a certain levity (the more severe might call it flippancy) in places. Put it down to my character and temperament. I am not, in the conventional sense of the term, a pious man. I take comfort from the fact that neither was Luther, if some passages of his *Table Talk* are any indication. I do not believe my task as a preacher is to commend what is pious but to

12

state what is true in the only way I know how—as a down-to-earth Lancastrian often more at home in the company of the Godless than in the fellowship of the Saints. Albeit, I accept without reservation the existence of saints as the final proof of the truth of Christianity. But I am not amongst their number—a comment based not on false humility but cold self-knowledge. Hence, I can only preach to the limits of my faith and offer an exposition of preaching which makes no claims I am unable to substantiate from personal experience.

Whilst I am at the business of spiritual striptease, let me confess with candour that I possess no mystical streak in my nature. When asked to meditate in silence on the ineffable glory of God, I tend to nod off or fidget in impatience. And when invited by a preacher to be still and concentrate on the presence of God, I find myself irreverently conjecturing precisely what or who is passing through the minds of the rest of the congregation. The hardness of the pews rather than the grandeur of the Almighty seems to impinge upon my consciousness. The corollary of this waywardness is that I can count on the fingers of both hands the number of sermons I have preached which might be described as being of a devotional nature. So this dimension of preaching is missing from the book because it is lacking in my religious experience.

Someone whose judgement I value has commented that the manuscript lacks the strong emphasis on Christian political and social action which has, for better or worse, been the style of ministry with which I am associated. The point is well taken. My only possible riposte is to ask that this book should be read in conjunction with others I have written, not in the comparative tranquillity of my London study but from the heart of the freedom struggle of the African continent. This is not a 'plug' aimed at increasing my sales but a recognition that no work on preaching could possibly contain chapters on 'Martyrdom and How I Attained It' or 'Congregations—Techniques for Losing Them', with an Appendix on 'How to Provoke Detractors into Blowing Up One's Church'.

Every honest preacher will experience his Mount of Transfiguration, walk with leaden steps to a private Golgotha, and, hopefully, emerge from the tomb into the Garden of Resurrection. I do not believe that a re-enactment of the Passion of Christ can be contrived. This book is not a training manual for putative prophets or miniscule messiahs perversely seeking unoccupied crosses on which to impale themselves. It is enough to preach the Word with integrity and one will find it impossible to escape both the suffering and glory of the Cross.

A final point which some might regard as trivial. I have throughout referred to the preacher as being of the masculine gender. I am well aware that some of the most effective preachers of our day are women, and I would not insult them by adding that footnote which appears in too many of our liturgical offices—'The masculine is taken to imply the feminine where appropriate'. On different grounds I find the term 'person' intolerably impersonal, and syntactically the substitution of 'he or she' for 'him' fouls my verbs up to the point where I am in a grammatical maze out of which I cannot extricate myself without disrupting the rhythm of my sentences. I prefer to come clean in the belief that all but the most obsessive Women's Libbers will sympathize with my difficulties and accept that there is no disrespect intended either to their sex or vocation as preachers. If that is a vain hope, then my sincere apologies and the assurance, which I trust will be accepted, that no sexual discrimination is implied.

I am deeply conscious of the honour of being the first Englishman to deliver the Voigt Lectures on Preaching, following such great American preachers as Dr George A. Butterick and Bishop Gerald Kennedy. I also used some of the material at the Iliff School of Theology in Denver, Colorado. I skirted round the edges of the same theme in the Frank S. Hickman Lectures on Ministry at Duke University, Durham, N. Carolina. I trust that my repeated treatment of this subject will not be interpreted as a shortage of new ideas but more as evidence of my conviction that it is vital for the Church to rediscover the central significance of preaching in its life.

COLIN MORRIS

London
November 1974

CONTENTS

ONE

The Word—Debased yet Revalued

EVERY Sunday throughout the Christian world, millions of words are spoken in the course of what many people within the Church and outside it regard as a parody of true communication—the sermon. And there is little point in traditional Christians commenting sniffily that if the public at large do not appreciate the importance of preaching then so much the worse for them. There *is* a crisis centring on the pulpit which must be honestly faced. Many theological students, for instance, treat lectures on the art of preaching almost as casually as those charged to teach them the subject.

Certainly the storm which now rages about the effectiveness of preaching has been brewing for a long time. When Bishop Matthew Simpson, who gave Abraham Lincoln's funeral address, delivered the Lyman-Beecher Lectures on Preaching at Yale in 1879, his final lecture was significantly titled 'Is the Modern Pulpit a Failure?' He answered his own question with a distinction which contemporary critics might think disingenuous. . . . 'There is a definite difference between failure in the pulpit and the failure of the pulpit itself. A cook may be a failure, but the kitchen remains an imperative necessity.' Such a judgement shows commendable modesty on the preacher's part but also accepts

19

unreservedly the validity of what he is doing when he mounts the pulpit steps.

This is the rub. Neither the preacher's motive nor his competence is necessarily under challenge. It is the sermon itself as a method of communication which is widely discounted either as an old-fashioned or even counterproductive way of confronting people with the Gospel.

John Ruskin defined a sermon as 'thirty minutes in which to raise the dead'. Few preachers in our day would make such a breathtaking claim for it, if only because not many erstwhile spiritual corpses stride out of our churches, vibrant with new life as a consequence of a process of resuscitation that has taken place between the third and fourth hymns. Latter-day Lazaruses are thin on the ground. The average preacher, far from raising the dead, is well content if he succeeds in waking those who sleep.

Ruskin's definition takes us into very deep water. It might be prudent to begin by dipping our toe into the shallow end of the pool and exploring the more superficial reasons why preaching is currently devalued.

First, a statement of the obvious: all the activities of a shrinking Church tend to contract proportionately in the attention given to them. Empty pews, declining membership, financial and manpower crises are not conducive to powerful preaching. This argument can be stood on its head and often is by zealous Christians who claim that the Church would not be shrinking if the quality of preaching were better. The weight of evidence, however, does not support this contention. Some of the most gifted preachers of our day are unable to maintain, let alone increase, the size of their congregations.

The drastic shift of emphasis from Church to action-orientated Christianity has also had its effect upon preaching. Parsons, particularly fiery young radicals, fully extended in community reform, working with movements aimed at attacking poverty, discrimination, bad housing and so forth, tend to put the rituals of the gathered Church fairly low on their list of priorities. Some of them give a grudging couple of hours of a Saturday evening to sermon preparation, in contrast to the pulpit giants of the past who locked themselves in their studies every week-day morning and laboured at desks groaning under the weight of Biblical Commentaries and Concordances, polishing homiletical gems for the following Sunday.

When conservatively inclined congregations regard the activities of a crusading parson with varying degrees of disapproval if not downright suspicion, he may reach a point of despair where he feels that he has nothing to say to them other than 'May the Lord have mercy upon you!'—a sentiment heartily reciprocated by his people. Having survived decades of thunderous pulpit declamation without showing any signs of change other than those ravages of age which cause them to sit ever nearer the back of the church the deafer they get, some congregations strike a parson dumb by their obduracy.

Let a preacher exhort his people to join him in the struggle for social justice, look back and find himself marching alone, then it demands almost superhuman forbearance to avoid using the pulpit to purvey Good Chidings rather than Good Tidings. The sermon becomes a twenty-minute tirade which the congregation endure with a stoicism born of long practice, except of course for the minority who get perverse enjoyment out of the conviction that the preacher's sharper verbal shafts are aimed at the man or woman in the next pew. It is part of the cherished store of theological students' mythology that there are so many bald-headed men in church because the preacher's lash never gets further than scalp-deep before it is deftly deflected elsewhere.

Traditional preaching also suffered during the harrowing the Church underwent in the period of theological ferment characterized by the *Honest to God* and *Death of God* furores. A preacher privately wrestling with doubt is unlikely to proclaim publicly the so-called certainties of the Faith with much confidence. This is not to suggest that scholars such as Bishop John Robinson and Professor Thomas Altizer have done the Church any disservice by storming the citadels of traditional belief. Quite the contrary. The New Theology forced Christians to *think*—a task so uncongenial to some that they either left the Church altogether or else took themselves off to sit at the feet of preachers for whom Robinson is the name of a brand of barley water or possibly a synonym for the Devil.

It would be both silly and unjust to lay the blame for the decline in the Church's membership at the door of *avant garde* theologians. Sociologists were charting the drift away from organized religion long before the authors of *Honest to God* and *The Gospel of Christian Atheism* were old enough to spell the titles of their controversial books let alone develop the ideas they contain. Yet it would be idle to pretend that a period of profound theological questioning strengthens the authority of the pulpit, though it may in the long run improve the quality of the Church's life and witness. In the short term, the preacher of modest intellectual equipment may, wretched in his honesty, turn the sermon into a performance during which he wrestles with his personal doubts in front of an invited audience—as though they have not enough of their own!

In fact, the strongest challenge to the pulpit in this century did not originate within the Church at all but has been a spin-off from the revolution our society has undergone since the Second World War. The widespread availability of television in the Western world, for instance, has accustomed the public to *visual* rather than *verbal* statements of truth, half-truth and downright lie. During the twenty-five years that the television set has been transformed from a luxury to a necessity of conventional civilized living, a whole world of realism and fiction has impinged on the consciousness of the masses in an explosion of multi-coloured pictures emanating from the corner of their living rooms.

One of the most perceptive of TV critics, Peter Black, has argued that television is not so much a window as a mirror, reflecting rather than illuminating the human condition:

> Television has become a huge and intractable medium that offers problems but no solutions, questions but no answers, plenty of ifs and buts but no therefores. . . . Belief in television's influence is rather like belief in life after death. Most of us would like to be able to prove it, but evidence is inconclusive. What began as a window on the world is now seen, more truly, as the reflection of it; and to suppose that you can change society by changing the television programmes is like supposing that you can alter a face by distorting a mirror.[1]

Such a conclusion may comfort verbal communicators and enrage moralists seeking a rectangular scapegoat for the escalation in violence, greater permissiveness and the subversion of parliamentary democracy by widespread riot and demonstration in our society. The preacher, however, is less likely to be reassured. It is the medium not the message —to maul Marshall McLuhan's epigram which has become a dog-eared cliché—that concerns him as he engages in the task of re-assessing his craft. If it is the Image rather than the Word which speaks to our generation then his future is somewhat bleak unless he can as an old dog learn new tricks and abandon oratory for film projection or drama production.

Wishful thinking it may be, but currently I detect signs that the public who once watched television with total absorption from the moment the station came on the air until it closed down in the early hours of the following

[1] Black, *The Mirror in the Corner*, p. 217 (Hutchinson, 1972)

morning are becoming more discriminating in their viewing. They have discovered that most blessed of inventions, the switch. The day of the spoken word may once more be dawning. It will be truly ironic if there is no one left to speak it.

Oratory of all kinds, long ailing, has become a dead art during the years television sets, if not the locusts, have eaten. What cannot be expressed in half a dozen crisp sentences, interrupted three times by a belligerent TV interviewer who appears to have a paranoid urge to get on to the next item in the programme, is not truth. The Gospel is not susceptible of such treatment. I do not mean that it is, or ought to be beyond the challenge of any interrogator on TV or elsewhere. But it must be stated before it can be confuted. And this may take longer than the producer's stop-watch will allow.

Television is one of the innumerable achievements of a highly advanced technological society. There have also been casualties, of which language is the most serious. Formulae, diagrams and models are the encapsulated truths of Scientific Man. Lamentably, it is possible to earn and win a Nobel Prize in some abstruse scientific field without being able to put together a dozen grammatical sentences for the purposes of one's acceptance speech. Language has thinned out until it is as insipid as workhouse gruel. If the present trend continues, we shall soon be communicating with one another by means of grunts like the Stone Age denizens of a centrally heated, air-conditioned cave.

The specialization which is the fruit of technology has turned our society into a second Tower of Babel where men can only communicate with their own kind in the argot of a private freemasonry. There is a certain grisly truth in the story of the two psychiatrists who meet in the street. One says, 'Good morning!' The other muses, 'I wonder what he meant by *that*?'

24

When scientific specialization has almost reached the point where a different surgeon is required to remove each tonsil, a key question hangs in the air of our time. When the specialists have taken Man apart, who is to put him together again? Who will see him steadily and whole as a person who lives, loves, sins and dies? I would contend that it is the preacher and only the preacher who addresses Man in his wholeness, the totality of his being. In this world of specialists, the preacher is an unashamed generalizer. With breathtaking audacity, he states truths which are cosmic in sweep and yet apply to any individual, anywhere at any time.

All very true, you may concede, but no analysis of why preaching is at a discount can rehabilitate it. No human power or wit can rehabilitate it at all. Only God can do that. God plus the mystery of the moment, for what Victor Hugo claimed for an idea whose time has come—that it is mightier than any army—equally applies, I suspect, to the word of the preacher. When a man, his truth and the moment come into providential conjunction then out of their union the explosive force of the Eternal Spirit ignites a holy flame which may run like a brush fire throughout a society and an historical epoch.

Has this power deserted God's Church? Will men never again echo the words of Thomas Randolph who said of John Knox's sermons, 'They put more spirit in us than the sound of five hundred trumpets blustering in our ears'? Dare we believe with that other John Robinson, of Leyden, 'God has yet more light and truth to break forth from his Holy Word'? Is it possible that men of Essex might do as their forebears did who flocked to hear John Rogers, one of the great Puritan preachers roaring like a lion from a country pulpit?—'Let us go to Dedham,' they said, 'to get a little fire.' Could any twentieth-century Wesley have Cornish tin miners break into tears of contrition and gratitude?

Of course there were giants abroad in those days. And it is wisdom to heed the words of the Jewish rabbi who said that God never does the same thing twice—which presumably includes reincarnating the pulpit princes of the past. Yet if preaching *is* finished then so is the Church, for preaching founded it, carried it to the far corners of the earth and has sustained it in existence, battered, diminished and humbled as it may be, to this day.

I am not concerned with what I would call the nuts and bolts of preaching—sermon construction, voice production and the like. To be honest, such an approach to the subject has a lack of fascination all its own for me. I believe that technique can only develop out of a profound understanding of what preaching is, and will reflect the nuances, the strengths and weaknesses, of the preacher's personality and the balance of his gifts.

Hence, I have chosen to approach the subject crab-wise, attempting to examine the paradoxes which seem to me inherent in preaching. In order to impose some structure on my ideas, I have borrowed, with consent, the title of Dr Gordon Rupp's 1972 Diamond Jubilee Lecture of the London Baptist Preachers' Association—'The Word and the Words'—and used variations of it as chapter headings. For it is the many ways in which the Eternal Word inheres and occasionally bursts out of our human words that give life to this strange activity we call preaching.

TWO

The Word—Inadequate yet Eventful

1 *The Inadequate Word*

It goes without saying that the inadequate Word is ours
and not God's. Preaching is not difficult: it is strictly
impossible. The man who launches himself from a tall
building, flapping plywood wings, may be regarded by
amused onlookers as a crank; in fact, his aim—to soar like
a bird without outside propulsion—is child's play compared
with the goal set for the preacher. There is more chance of
splitting the atom with a feather duster than preaching an
adequate sermon. Why? Because preaching is the attempt to
communicate by the crude, inexact medium of words the
essence of the ultimate Mystery—God.

Isaiah put it in one memorable phrase, 'Truly, you are a
God who hides yourself!' And so say all of us! Or at least
most of us. There *are* preachers who chat about God with a
folksy familiarity that is breathtaking. They would be
modest enough to confess they haven't the foggiest idea
what is going on in the head of their family pet but lay
claim to sure knowledge of what their Pal Up There is
thinking about the National Economy, the Middle East
conflict or even the future of Mankind.

Most theologians, having had the benefit of a university

education, wouldn't quarrel with Isaiah: they just say the same thing in longer words. God is not a secular reality, defining 'secular' as that area of knowledge and experience intelligible to the human mind. Charles Davis puts it well:

> Mystery is the presence of God. Man cannot with truth locate that presence. God is not beyond or outside the world; he is not above or below; he is neither within nor without. He is an undefined presence, which imposes itself upon man's experience without uncovering the secret of Divine Being.[1]

The claim that God is mysterious does not mean his essence lies beyond the present frontiers of knowledge, with the implication that sooner or later these frontiers will be pushed back to reveal what is presently hidden. God is not unknown. He is unknowable. The mystery in which he shrouds himself is not like a blanket of fog which the fresh winds of new truth will one day disperse.

Obviously, if God *were* a secular reality—one Object, however awesome, in the world of the senses—faith would be of little significance if not entirely superfluous. It does not take much faith to believe in the existence of Westminster Abbey. If I myself had not seen it, then I would certainly have to trust the word of someone who had, or accept that any photographs of it were genuine. But in the last resort, to doubt its existence would put a question mark against my sanity rather than its reality. Because God's Being eludes the senses, the preacher is not an educator, passing on to students things *he* knows which *they* do not. He deals in faith; his own and that which he hopes to engender in his hearers. But he needs help, the ultimate help—God's self-disclosure in revelation. And even here, his best efforts are inadequate, for he not only sees through a glass darkly but has limited means at his disposal to tell of what he has seen.

[1] Charles Davis, *God's Grace in History* (Sheed & Ward, 1966)

Hence, all preachers are, in Paul's words, true deceivers. They have more in common with artists than scientists. The painter must deliberately use symbolism which conveys how things appear rather than how they actually are in order to overcome the problem of recording two dimensions of space on the single dimension of canvas. The scientist knows, and our common sense tells us, that parallel lines never meet. Yet whenever an artist paints a street scene from a certain angle, the parallel rows of houses on each side of a straight road *do* meet in the far distance. A child, on the other hand, who knows nothing of the laws of perspective, tells the truth. He draws two parallel rows of houses which do not converge on the horizon. From the stance of the viewer, the child's truth is lie whilst the artist's deception is truth.

In the same way, the preacher must ransack his mind and vocabulary for images and illustrations which do not in the strict sense convey truth but may communicate some aspect of God's Being which is beyond the reach of the senses. He must sacrifice fact to meaning as, for instance, when he claims God is our Father. As a matter of *fact*, such an assertion is utterly absurd in any historical sense and can be disproved detail by detail. Yet as an analogy, the term 'Father' is as near as one can get to the fundamental truth about God's relationship with mankind.

Trinity Sunday is the preacher's Waterloo. If he is prudent he will go down with a strategic bout of influenza the preceding day. If he suffers from a stern sense of duty, he will be forced to tie himself in verbal knots grappling with the ultimate mystery of God's Nature. Indeed, the Church could make an honest penny charging militant atheists an admission fee for the pleasure of seeing and hearing Christian preachers battle their way through an intellectual maze, which, at whatever point they enter it, soon has them hopelessly lost. This is the one Sunday of the Christian Year when the organist cannot afford to doze gently through the sermon, for he never knows when he will have to answer the preacher's distress signal by playing the opening bars of the final hymn—preferably *double forte*—to drown out the sound of groans of exhaustion from the pulpit.

Yet let the honest preacher take comfort from the fact that however pathetic his efforts to proclaim the Trinity, the Fathers of the Church did not do much better. To plough one's way through the majestically opaque language of the Athanasian Creed, a literary quagmire if ever there was one, is to realize with some relief that God must have a sense of humour and delight in cutting down to size the theological giants of the Church.

The doctrine of the Trinity is probably the most conclusive example of the futility of trying to rationalize a mystery; to imprison God in a web of words; to pin him down like a specimen butterfly in a show-case. But which basic Christian doctrine has not mystery at its heart? Incarnation, Atonement, Resurrection, Ascension, Consummation, can only be articulated by doing violence to both language and logic. The entire Christian Faith is predicated upon an intellectual absurdity—the idea of eternity entering time. That which is eternal is unconditional, without beginning or end, completely untouched and unchanged by the contingencies of history. That which is of time is subject to growth and decay, birth and death, beginning and end. In the words of Reinhold Niebuhr: 'The truth that the Word was made flesh outrages all the canons by which truth is usually judged. Yet it is the truth. The whole character of the Christian religion is involved in that affirmation.'[2]

The mysterious element in the Faith is bound to give a preacher the desperate feeling of trying to capture waves in

[2] R. Niebuhr, *Beyond Tragedy* (Books for Libraries Press, 1937)

a fishing net. That reality which is inexpressible will burst out of any combination of words the wit of man can put together. But we compound the felony by our slovenly and slap-dash way with language. Of all the bewildering variety of skills a technological society has developed, the ability to know the weight of a word is among the rarest. Few speakers and preachers of our day seem to have such a feeling for the cadence of language that a dissonant word jars like a badly tuned fiddle in an orchestra, or to use a simile more in keeping with the contemporary spirit, like the sudden clatter in a smoothly purring automobile engine.

I am neither commending nor defending 'preachy' language—that portentousness of expression often garnished with a superficial ornateness which hides aridity of thought. I happen to believe that grammar and syntax were not invented to torment little boys and girls. The correct way of saying something is invariably the most lucid and clearly understood expression of the underlying idea. And if that idea should be of life- or world-transforming power, as are the truths of the Gospel, it is surely the sin for which there shall be no forgiveness for a preacher to neglect the sacred ministry of style—hard labour aimed at producing a blend of beauty, strength and simplicity that characterize the English language at its best.

Let me hasten to add that I by no means belittle those preachers who have learned the colourful in-language of youth and have a flair for socking the Gospel to 'em. But it *is* a flair. Young people have an unerring instinct for the condescension which is implied in a self-conscious mateyness and rightly reject the blandishments of middle-aged clerical teeny-boppers.

The preacher's language ought to reflect the significance of what he is doing, and the dignity of it. Even though it is by definition impossible to explain what is mysterious, language ought at least to reflect the awesomeness of that mystery. Nor should we forget that it is possible to reduce the dimensions of a truth by attempting too tight a definition of it. That great American preacher, Dr Phillips Brooks, was surely making the same point when he commented, 'When I am interesting I am vague, when I am definite I am dull'. Better by far to wrestle with a truth that defies definition than produce a definition devoid of truth—though one qualification is necessary. Obscurity should ·not be mistaken for profundity; the inexpressible is not the same as the unintelligible; verbal fog is not synonymous with ineffable glory. The congregation may have to be led to that 'thick darkness where God is' but if the preacher is doing his job they will sense *there* a transcendence which evokes adoration rather than reel from a miasma of words that leaves them hopelessly confused.

For all its importance, the preacher must not make *style*, verbal or literary, the be-all and end-all of true preaching. Nothing could be further from the truth; indeed, style must always be the servant of truth. In my experience, the greatest enemy of the spoken Word is sometimes the teacher of the spoken word—the expert in homiletics who puts together sermons like the bones of an articulated skeleton and encourages pulpit apprentices to do the same. The result is neat, perfectly jointed and very, very dead.

A recent television documentary dealt with the life and art of Picasso. At one point, the interviewer invited the great artist to demonstrate his genius. Unhesitatingly Picasso picked up a brush, dipped it into paint and in one continuous sweep drew a perfect circle on a blank canvas. Simplicity itself; yet a life-time of grinding labour, endless practice and total dedication were compressed into that single stroke. So it is with great preaching. The hearer is not moved to gasps of admiration at the preacher's ingenuity in taking some rarefied text and developing it into a miracle

of verbal felicity, point succeeding point in majestic progression to a triumphant conclusion. He is more likely
to snap his fingers in irritation and exclaim, 'Why didn't
I think of that?' or else, 'Precisely! That's how I've often
felt!'

The supreme characteristic of a great sermon is that
anyone *might* have preached it . . . *might* have done, but it
took a great preacher to do it. Like Picasso's perfect circle,
it is style in the service of truth. Anyone with a modicum of
fluency and a gift for words can try to express the inexpressible in a torrent of ideas tumbling over one another in
images and illustrations. The ultimate pulpit skill is to state
a truth simply without denuding it of mystery. That, as the
punters would say, is a horse of a different colour. And the
professor of theology has no edge on the farm labourer
who left school at fourteen and stumbles and stutters
his way to that 'thick darkness where God is'. The ultimate
test is—which one takes the congregation along with
him?

But both professor of theology and farm labourer are up
against the same insuperable problem—the inadequacy of
words as all-too fragile bearers of the weight of Mystery.
Yet let every preacher take heart from the fact that
Shakespeare wrote over 150 sonnets attempting to capture
the essence of Love in words and had to confess his failure.
But he made beautiful music in the process. Possibly that is
the best the greatest preacher can do—fail magnificently and
in so doing testify to the glory of the God who eludes him
in his eloquence and yet is hauntingly present in his
silences.

Who and What God is in himself remains inscrutable, yet
he teases, tantalizes and attracts us by the way he flits
through the world of our senses. Plato talked of fleeting
shadows in a cave; Paul saw baffling reflections in a mirror;
a Hebrew poet described the 'whisper of God's ways'—the

rustle of his garments as he walked through the Garden in the cool of the day. And at this point language breaks down.

2 *The Eventful Word*

If matters rested there, the most eloquent, indeed the *only* valid testimony of God's Being within institutional religion would be an empty pulpit and a silent preacher. In fact, some preachers, convinced that matters *do* rest there, have exchanged their Geneva gowns for multi-hued copes and seek to convey the essence of the mystery which eludes their words in the ceremonials of altar and font. It is not entirely fortuitous that the decline in preaching has coincided with a growth in sacerdotalism.

Certainly we Protestants, if one is permitted that old-fashioned term in the Age of Ecumenism, have a built-in tendency to under-value the sacramental ministry—but about that more anon. Meanwhile, it must be roundly stated that the Sacrament of the Word is *the* primary sacrament. It stands over the so-called Dominical Sacraments, both embracing and sanctioning them, even as the Eucharist and Baptism in turn proclaim the Gospel. Those who are of the spiritual lineage of Luther and Wesley dare not forget that the preacher is a sacramental person. He must not sell short his heritage for a dollop of sacerdotal pottage as colourful as candy floss and just about as nourishing.

Anyway, it is faulty thinking and bad theology to set action against words; to claim a special authenticity for something done rather than said. For what is Holy Communion without the Words of Institution—however dramatically the priest tears apart the bread or wafer? And what an eccentricity is Baptism unless it is anchored firmly within the Christian tradition by the specific statement that it is done at our Lord's command!

34

However, beyond noting that the Dominical Sacraments are inextricably linked with preaching and are not substitutes for it, we cannot for the moment take this matter further. The key issue remains. The preacher's word *is* inadequate and neither an improved vocabulary nor a louder voice can remedy the deficiency.

As so often in human life, it is precisely at the point of our despair that God comes to our rescue and turns preaching into an act of revelation. The preacher's words become eventful because they are charged with living truth. It is by Divine intervention and not human ingenuity that preaching must be accounted a unique activity, totally set apart from other 'wordy' crafts such as oratory or teaching, though a sermon may contain elements of both. But neither a man's way with words nor his gift for communicating knowledge is a skill of the same order as preaching. And it is important to try to define the difference, even if it defies logic.

The words which make up preaching are not descriptions of some truth: they *are* that truth. This is a strictly religious phenomenon. Obviously in everyday life, the words which describe a sunset are not that sunset; they are an attempt to recreate in the hearer one's own sense of the grandeur and beauty of an experience. But the realm of revelation has its own laws, one of which concerns the form and method of communicating truth. John Austin Baker, in one of the most important and under-publicized theological works of our time, *The Foolishness of God*, makes this perceptive comment on the exposition of Scripture:

> There is a simple fact which is often forgotten, namely that thoughts (other than mathematical ones) are not *expressed* in words—they *exist* in words and only in words. When we are reading the words of an ancient culture, therefore, we are reading their thoughts, their concept of the truth . . . truth does not come to men clothed in words, it comes to them as

35

words; and when as far as possible we know what the words meant to them, then as far as possible we know what the truth was to them.[3]

And what applies to the interpretation of ancient religious writings is equally relevant to our preaching. Our words *are* our thoughts and hopefully God's too.

But I would go even further and claim that when the Word is proclaimed, words become events—a localized Genesis has taken place. In the Biblical account of Creation, there is no suggestion that God *did* anything. He spoke and something happened—'God said, Let there be Light, and there was Light.' Intention and execution are a union cemented by God's word. Hence, allowing with due modesty for the fact that few preachers imagine they are recreating the Cosmos in the twenty minutes or so allotted to the sermon, preaching is, in the slang of our time, a 'happening' rather than a performance.

What, then is happening? Nothing less than an act of Divine revelation. And revelation is not the uncovering of truths beyond the range of human ingenuity. Revelation is the self-bestowal of God. Hence, no preacher with a true awareness of what he is doing will approach his task with any attitude other than a sense of awe far removed from the chirpy chattiness or false certitude of much that passes for modern preaching.

Need one add that the God who revealed himself through a Galilean peasant is capable of using little words and simple sentences as vehicles of his self-bestowal? Awe rarely issues in sententiousness and never in sanctimoniousness. It is not the monopoly of the theologian whose occupational disease is to deal in holy ideas with such habitual ease that any awe he is capable of evincing tends to be reserved for theologians more eminent than himself. Nor is it the posture of the 'Preacher' (encased in inverted commas and preceded by a

[3] J. A. Baker, *The Foolishness of God* (John Knox Press, 1975)

capital P) who is often so enraptured with the elegance of his sermonic structure and the ingenuity of his textual exposition that the sermon becomes a self-justifying exercise in professional brilliance. Where there is no awe there is no revelation and where there is no revelation there is no true preaching of the Word.

I am well aware that such a high view of preaching is likely to be dismissed as old-fashioned and jejune. So be it. I do not gain the impression that those who dismiss preaching as having had its day are exactly revitalizing the Church let alone confronting society with its Lord with any marked degree of success.

Without apology therefore, I would put the stakes still higher and claim for preaching a role in God's providential care of the world breathtaking in its implications. When the Word is truly preached—and that adverb will need closer definition later—the congregation do not merely hear of the Christ-Event, they become part of it. Nor is the preacher proclaiming the story of the Incarnation, he is perpetuating it. Testimony to the Christ-Event conveys the essence of the personhood of Jesus to the extent God, in the sovereign freedom of the Spirit, wishes it to be known. But the emphasis in definition reflects the source of the initiative—God's use of our words not to dispel mystery but to illuminate it.

Preaching is, therefore, both an appalling responsibility and an undeserved privilege. Is it any wonder that our Fathers talked of the 'call to preach' in hushed tones? Clerical young bloods may scoff and *avant garde* theologians deride but they would be hard put to deny that older generations of Christians may have been wrong about many things but not in their insistence that the proclamation of the Word was, potentially, an event of a life-changing and society-challenging significance. Congregations, whether they numbered ten or ten thousand, were expectant, ready to have their imagination fired, their faith tested, their spirit nerved. Anton Rubinstein, the nineteenth-century piano virtuoso, on tour in New York, asked if he would like to go to church, replied, 'Yes, if you can take me to a preacher who will tempt me to do the impossible!' Truly, the blight of small expectation has done even more damage to the structure of the Church than all the storms of empty rhetoric!

THREE

The Word—Personal yet Corporate

1 *The Personal Word*

IT is no longer mandatory in some of Britain's modern universities for the chair in Theology to be held by a professing Christian. I recently heard a lecture given by one of the new breed of Biblical teachers who is an honest agnostic. It was an odd experience. His scholarship was meticulous and he had obviously forgotten more about the New Testament than I shall ever know. He brought to his work a sense of detachment, of objectivity, which in any other academic discipline would be applauded as the epitome of true learning. He was as clinical as a pathologist doing a post-mortem on a corpse identifiable only by the label affixed to its big toe.

I learned much, but what I missed was a sense of theology as 'an act of adoration fraught with the risk of blasphemy'— to quote an *Expository Times* editorial on Paul Tillich. I could not help recalling that eminent scholar, T. W. Manson, who often began a lecture at a measured pace, exploring briskly some aspect of Biblical terrain, then imperceptibly his steps would quicken as he took wings and flew—teaching had been transformed into preaching as he crossed the barrier which separates scholarship from testimony.

The Gospel must not only be true but true for me if I am to preach it with conviction. It was, I think, Bishop Quayle, the pulpit titan of America's Mid West, who commented that preaching is not the art of making a sermon and delivering it but of making a preacher and delivering that. A neatly turned aphorism containing enough truth to launch the putative preacher on an exercise in self-examination. For what is in the sermon must be in the preacher first. The Gospel does not exist *in vaccuo*, it is incarnate in a person. That is how the strange story of Christianity began; that is how it survives today—by God's truth taking up residence in someone's mind and heart, claiming him, setting him apart and, in effect saying , 'Stand by me, live and if necessary die for me!'

Making personal experience a basic criterion by which true preaching is judged is to run the risk of an unhealthy and cramped subjectivism. No preacher can live more than one life, experience more than a finite number of situations, know more things than one brain can contain. So from his own resources he cannot speak to the clamant needs of any congregation, however small it may be. Hence, the Church. . . .

The Church is the greatest preacher in Christian history and the individual preacher preaches *to* the Church from the Gospel in order that he may preach *from* the Church to the world. Put differently: the preacher can only preach beyond his own experience when he is preaching out of the Church's. And what a rich tapestry can be woven from the history of the universal Church! Could anything befall mortal man that the Church has not known? Bane and blessing, pain and pleasure, glory and defeat, humiliation and vindication, betrayal and forgiveness—the Church has lived through the totality of human experience. So the preacher's 'We' is neither editorial nor royal; it is confessional. 'Were you there when they crucified my Lord?'

asks the spiritual. To which the preacher can answer 'Yes!';
and when the Holy Spirit in tongues of flame licked a motley
assembly at Pentecost into shape—the form of the primitive
Church; *and* at every historical crisis precipitated by the
Gospel ever since.

Hence, there must always be a dialectical relationship
between the preacher and the Church. He can attack or
defend it, but in the last resort he must affirm it. Sometimes
the preacher's attitude towards the Church may be one of
questioning or even disillusionment; at others, his understanding of the Gospel may lead him to repudiate it. But the
tension is always there. The Church haunts the heretic as
the memory of home teases the Prodigal. It is the datum-
point, the landmark on the map from which the preacher
gets his bearings. The Church and the preacher's need of
each other is mutual. In the preacher, the Church becomes
conscious of itself. In the Church, the preacher draws upon
a fount of living faith immeasurably greater than his
own.

It is necessary to make large claims for the Church in an
age when even Christians devalue it, but we must not lose
our sense of proportion. The Church may license a preacher
but it does not call him. That authority comes from God
alone. The Church provides the preacher with a pulpit; it
is the living coals from off its altar which touch his lips,
purge his sins and take away his iniquity so that he can speak
those terrifying words of surrender and self-abnegation,
'Lord, here I am . . .'. Though the Church may be the
guardian of that altar flame, it is the Spirit of God which
fuels it. In the last resort, the preacher is the servant of the
Word and not the lackey of the Community the Word calls
into existence.

I must interpose here a comment about the preacher's
personal word which may seem to some gratuitously
insulting or even cruel. Yet it must be stated. If, as is often

claimed, our sin crucifies Jesus afresh, then without doubt it is our mediocrity which buries him again. I have a theory, or at least a hypothesis which admits of many exceptions, but is still worth putting to the test of individual experience —*boring sermons are generally the product of dull personalities.* To be sure, I have known men who were mice in their private lives but roared like lions in the pulpit. By some strange alchemy, their tin whistles were transmuted into trumpets the moment they mounted those steps. And they gave forth no uncertain sound.

And yet . . . as a rough rule of thumb it is those who strike one in casual encounter as 'characters' who bring to the pulpit colour and vigour in their preaching. In the words of John Henry Jowett, delivering the Lyman-Beecher Lectures at Yale in 1912:

> Reverently respect your own individuality. I do not advise you to be aggressively singular, for then you may stand revealed as a crank, and your influence will be gone. But without being angular believe in your own angle and work upon the assumption that it is through your own unrepeated personality that God purposes that your light should break upon the world. Reverently believe in your own uniqueness. . . .[1]

Many great preachers were choc-a-bloc with idiosyncracies to the point of eccentricity. Henry Ward Beecher, Joseph Parker, Dean Inge, P. T. Forsyth and that majestic succession of Scottish divines ranging from Alexander Whyte to Professor James Moffatt—each has been a rich source of anecdote, apocryphal or otherwise; their sayings and doings, their habits and quirks reveal them to have been personalities constructed on a grand scale. As a necessary corrective one must mention preachers every bit as gifted but more conventional in life-style; for instance, H. H. Farmer, Leslie Weatherhead, James S. Stewart. Conventional but certainly not dull.

[1] J. H. Jowett, *The Preacher: His Life and Work*, p. 128 (New York, 1912)

There is a serious principle at stake here. Of course we cannot all be ten-talent personalities, either in the pulpit or everyday life. Few are built to heroic proportions, and blame Nature for that, but the preacher has no excuse for mediocrity. Indeed, anyone who can contrive to make dull intelligence of the Good News of the Gospel has an inverted genius of sorts. Yet who has not known pulpiteers who could make the announcement of the Second Coming sound as pedestrian as a station-master broadcasting the approach of the 9.34 from Neasden? A commanding presence, a voice with the resonance and range of an organ, a mind able to cast fresh light on old truths and that instinctive sense of the weight of a word—these qualities are given to few. But no one *need* be mediocre. A dull personality is the end-product of mental laziness, spiritual lassitude and moral cowardice—a refusal to take risks in relationships.

Words are the preacher's basic tool and a preacher who does not read to stretch his vocabulary and give house-room to new ideas is like a professional pianist whose repertoire is confined to 'Chop-Sticks' and 'God Save the Queen'. Dullness is a form of egotism—lack of curiosity about God's world and the people to be encountered in it. There is, alas, such a thing as a parsonical life-style which can be passed down from generation to generation like an inherited abnormality. Goodness degenerates into conventionality, self-discipline into timidity, wit atrophies for lack of exercise and gives place to an hearty bonhommie. Those angularities of personality which make us both different from and interesting to our fellowmen are rubbed smooth by the abrasive effect of one bland individual endlessly rebounding off others of like mind and constitution.

I hope the element of parody in this depiction of the archetypal parson may be forgiven me. It is intended more as a warning than an exact description. But at risk of disloyalty to my fellow Christians I must confess to a secret wish that the naturally nice people in the Church were 'salted' with more nasty ones of ability who could in truth say, 'If you think I'm a bad lot now, you should have met me before Christ took hold of me!' However, that is, as the music-hall comedians would say, a throw-away line. Back to my main theme with one last comment on the preacher's personality.

As one who is jealous for the power and authority of the pulpit, I can only record with regret my fear that the preacher's mouthpiece seems to have become the parrot's bill instead of the eagle's beak. I readily confess that I view with some nostalgia the day when a Whitfield could declaim, 'The Angel of Death is beating his wings about us!' and there were those in the congregation who fainted away with shock. *Any* reaction other than a yawn or a glassy stare must be accounted a victory nowadays.

What is not a matter of nostalgia but an empirical fact is that in post-Christian Britain, preachers who are simply wizards of words rarely draw the crowds. The personal word has to become incarnate in action to command the attention of a sceptical society. Martin Luther King, Daniel Berrigan, Mother Teresa, Trevor Huddleston, Toyohiko Kagawa were or are heard eagerly because each one suffered for what he or she believed. When the crunch came, they were prepared to lay their lives on the line. So at a time when the pulpit has lost its traditional inherited authority, the preacher must bring to it his own brand of authenticity.

St Thomas is the patron saint of an Age which, in effect, says 'Don't tell us. Show us!' And who can blame those who, unless they can thrust their hands into the wounds we have sustained for Christ's sake, will not believe? False messiahs bawl their wares from every street corner. Hence, it is not from a pulpit but a cross that power-filled words are spoken. Sermons need to be seen as well as heard to be effectual. Eloquence, homiletical skill, Biblical knowledge are not enough. Anguish, pain, engagement, sweat and blood punctuate the stated truths to which men will listen.

To summarize this business of the peculiarly personal nature of the preacher's word: the eighth deadly sin is to profess publicly what one neither believes nor practises privately and for which there is no standing ground in the experience of the Church as a whole. Better by far the simple evangelist stammering out the story of his own conversion than the slick rhetorician borrowing the experience of others, and polishing and refining it until it takes away the congregation's breath by its virtuosity. For sure it will never take away their sin.

Nor need one apologize for the repetitiousness of the limited but valid truth which is one's own. It was the great Socrates who when his hearers complained that he was always repeating himself replied, 'If I am asked what two and two makes, what can I answer but "four"?'

There is, in fact, a ninth deadly sin which must not be overlooked. No preacher has the right to insult the intelligence of his hearers. They may be a captive audience—at least on the first occasion he addresses them—but they quickly develop an unerring instinct for that verbosity which smothers a trivial truth in a torrent of words or the glibness which wraps up the great mysteries of life in neat syllogisms. Let no preacher be ashamed to confess that he has no answer to the vicious conundrum of Evil, the anguish of undeserved suffering or the way through that Veil which separates mortality from Eternity. A congregation will respect the preacher who wrestles with a giant issue, is thrown and confesses defeat. It has only contempt for the preacher who hammers a paltry matter into the ground and then preens himself on his triumph.

Honesty above all else is the essence of the preacher's personal word, with humility its offspring. Though he speaks with the tongues of men and of angels and has not honesty he has forfeited his right of entry into the pulpit. Let him use his talents selling hair restorer in the marketplace or as caller in a bingo hall.

We live in a time when the preacher is required to lay his integrity on the line with complete openness. He cannot hide behind the skirts of the bishops or the robes of the doctors. He cannot pick other men's flowers, deliver other men's sermons or recite other men's beliefs with any hope of carrying conviction. Because all Establishments are suspect and a deep rebelliousness is stirring within the spirit of Man, the authority of the preacher is closely bound up with his personal character. In one sense, he has not been sent from God with any message. He *is* the message—its weight is his weight, and its convincing power is in direct proportion to his spiritual and intellectual capacity to open himself to the Gospel.

Preachers who skip along the surface of life, dallying with ideas, weaving webs of words as fragile as gossamer even though they make pretty patterns, can neither know nor tell of the depths of Christ. And those whose *credo* is a thing of scissors and paste—snippets of biblical and theological gossip stuck together with the glue of holy unctuousness—will succeed only in fabricating a cardboard Jesus, destined to be blown away by the lightest breath of detractors.

2 *The Corporate Word*

As a balance to the notion that preaching is an intensely personal activity, it is necessary to invoke the other half of the paradox and emphasize the corporate Word. A preacher not only preaches *to* a congregation; he also preaches *out* of it. As Martin Luther put it, 'There can be no Word of God without the People of God'. The living word issues from a living community.

The preacher's truth must be his own, but this does not imply that it is no one else's. If his intention is to astound his hearers with propositions so novel they have hitherto been alien to human ears, then he is in the business of starting a new religion—in which case he has soared beyond the range of my argument. Otherwise, it is the preacher's task to give new life and urgency to truths that congregations have allowed through easy familiarity to sink into their collective unconscious.

According to Paul, the 'manifold wisdom of God is made known through the Church'. So behind the preacher's word is all the power of corporate conviction, the assurance of corporate faith and the impact of a corporate will. These are a few of the riches the Church offers the preacher. He in turn confronts the Church with itself—the actual with the ideal, the seen with the unseen, *a* church with *the* Church. He will not allow those who affirm Christ to meet negation with negation, declaring robustly to the sectarians who claim that there is no church but theirs, that theirs is no church of Christ. His churchmanship must be no less open than that of Jesus who said, 'Whosoever does the will of my Father who is in heaven, the same is my brother and sister and mother'.

John Wesley advised his followers to preach Christ in all his offices as Prophet, Priest and King. It is patently obvious that such an undertaking is beyond the intellect, dedication and wit of any individual, however gifted. The task belongs to the People of God because they are able to do together what none of them, including the man in the pulpit, could attempt in isolation. Wesley's dictum has its twentieth-century counterpart, a truism no doubt, but none the less true for that—only the whole Church can preach the whole Gospel to the whole World.

It is highly significant that at the climax of my Ordination Service, a bible was thrust into my hands and the words,

'Take thou authority to be a minister in the Church of God!'
were said over me. A single Denomination selects, trains
and employs the preacher, ministerial or lay, but his writ
runs throughout the Universal Church. Thus there is a
curious illogic in the exclusiveness of those Denominations
who will give the minister from outside access to
their pulpits but bar him from their altars. They have
swallowed a camel and strained at a gnat by failing to
recognize in preaching the supreme sacrament which
units the Church beyond the power of any sacerdotalism
to divide it.

So the preacher gathers up the experience of the People
of God, measures it against the Gospel and articulates it.
The preacher has spoken, but it is the Church which has
preached—and honesty compels one to admit that some of
its sermons can be both thin and dreary. For the Church is
made of the gritty stuff of the world; in fact, it *is* that bit of
the world shot through with the reconciling power of God.
One can, then, hardly be surprised at the Church's failures.
When it stumbles, the preacher falls flat on his face; its every
collective posture tends to throw into relief a characteristic
sin. A long time ago, an Irish-American preacher, J. Edgar
Park, addressed some blunt words to a class of theological
students:

> There is a curious connection between orthodoxy and mean-
> ness; evangelical rapture and financial untrustworthiness;
> liberalism and bigotry; temperance and gluttony; the expan-
> siveness of the pulpit and the constriction of personal
> generosity. An expert is 'an ordinary man away from home',
> and a saint's reputation too often depends upon the silence
> of his family.

Anyone care to argue?

Because the Church moulds and feeds the preacher, and
because the Church is fallible, there will be an inevitable

element of tension between the personal and corporate word. When in human terms, the People of God have conferred authority upon the preacher—and the Church's confidence in him may have to help him through many a situation where he has lost confidence in himself—that gift of authority is irrevocable. Once the people have given their sanction to a preacher, they cannot withdraw it if he should cease to please them. They have freed him from any grovelling subservience to their every whim and fancy. His is servanthood without servility. Far from conferring upon him a patronage which he holds at their will and pleasure, the people have given the preacher the power to stand up to them. They may repent at leisure of this magnanimity, especially if the preacher feels impelled to scarify their consciences rather than stroke their souls; but the deed has been done.

When Paul was brought before Agrippa and described his conversion, he claimed that God said to him on the Damascus Road, 'Stand on your feet, for I will make you a minister, *delivering you from the people*!' This is sometimes the preacher's greatest need—to be delivered from the people—who may smother him with kindness and trap him in a silken web of obligation so that it seems the basest ingratitude to stand against them with a word which cuts like a sword through the harmony and happy fellowship in which he has shared. However, let the reluctant controversialist take heart. Stephen, to our knowledge, only preached once and was greeted with a shower of stones for his trouble. Yet without that sermon there might have been no Paul.

Between the Church's corporate word and the preacher's personal one there may indeed be tension, yet more often the relationship is one of support and strength. For in the last resort the preacher is at the mercy of his people—a dependent man like his Lord who needed a human womb to carry him and a woman's breast at which to suck; he relied upon a father to shield him from Herod's wrath and friends to share his mission; he had to have one to help him carry his cross, and someone too, to roll away the stone from the entrance to his tomb. No preacher has the right to be ashamed of his vulnerability. Because he is expected to know more about the secret things of God than his hearers, it is one of the compensations of heavenly justice that he should be forced to rely upon their forbearance on his 'off-days', and their charity when his prophetic anger degenerates into unworthy scolding.

Herewith yet another of my scientifically unsubstantiated theories—in the last resort, congregations get the preachers they deserve. For who ministers to the one who ministers to them? At one level, I suppose it is the bishop or superintendent who is *pastor pastorum*, but in the week by week business of preaching, congregations have it within their power to make a preacher's ministry to them a radiant testimony or a pedestrian chore, if not a living hell.

How? Surely by reinforcing a preacher where he is weakest through their prayers and active encouragement and multiplying his strengths by their willingness to act upon his words.

Obviously no amount of congregational support can turn a sow's ear into a silk purse—Bill Bloggs into Leslie Weatherhead. Yet it can make the difference between failure and success, measured in the only terms that matter. I cannot claim to have studied the career of any lay preacher in great depth but I can certainly testify to the power of a congregation to sustain or destroy a ministry. I have known ministers, faithful and obedient men though undistinguished in the eyes of either Church or world, who exercised a powerful influence because their people sustained them. Other ministers of towering ability have crashed because the insensitivity or even hostility of their people has been like a leaden weight about their feet.

Assuming a necessary modicum of gifts and abilities in those whom the Church commissions to preach the Word, so pervasive is the mutuality between the preacher and his congregation that should the man in the pulpit prove a broken reed, the occupants of the pews would be wise to ask not 'Where did he go wrong?' but 'How did we fail him?'

What the Church *does* fundamentally affects what the preacher *says*. There are many definitions of Theology. The one I favour because it best anchors the subject in the real world is: theology as disciplined reflection upon the action of the People of God. Hence, if as is often alleged, contemporary theology is at a discount, it can only be because the People of God are not doing anything of much significance. And in the chain-reaction which follows, preaching will become trivialized and fussy, just as the dominant style of churchmanship will be neither high nor low, but thin—'bustle all week and baldness on Sunday' as P. T. Forsyth described the Church of his day, over half a century ago. And who dare claim things have got better; that the Church is heroically engaged, its preachers tackling great themes, challenging their hearers to attempt the impossible?

Let it be plainly stated: those who see the Church's salvation in terms of pulpit messianism—the Mighty Orator who, having taken up residence in the largest hall in the town, sweeps the masses off their feet by his perfervid rhetoric, are crying for the moon. It will not happen. And it cannot happen not merely because oratory is an ailing art but because only by entering into the fellowship of Christ's death can the Church enter into that Life which though eternal in quality is spent with utter prodigality upon the world. The theological radical finds the Church an embarrassment. So do we all. But let there be no mistake—the

Christian preacher, conservative or liberal, radical or evangelical, has no access to the world except through the Church. Not as a Christian. As a socialist, humanitarian, conservationist, idealist and political activist, possibly; but as a Christian preacher, never! In *that* role, he can act upon the world only through the Church and not as a substitute for it.

I believe the People of God are prior to both preacher and theologian; and this, not because they are morally more elevated or politically more engaged or spiritually more profound than other institutions of Man's devising. It just so happens that together they are the legatees of all the riches of God embodied in Christ. They are the Children of the Third Day—created by the Resurrection, empowered through Pentecost, the first fruits of that New Humanity which will inherit a New Heaven and Earth. I know of no logical reason why this should be so; certainly no ethical justification for it. Of all God's Mysteries, the Church is the most opaque to human reason. But it is *there* and unless God exercises his sovereign initiative to obliterate it and raise up some other instrument of his will, the preacher stands or falls by the Church—unless, of course, he falls outside it. In which case he can do as he likes; in fact, that is all he can do, as he likes.

Thus most preachers must articulate a corporate word and run for cover to the Church when the world turns upon them and challenges them to a verbal duel they are bound to lose. There will always be superb exceptions to the rule— preachers whose skills are the product of heredity—Mighty Men of the Word whose virtuosity leaves us gasping. They are God's gift to the Church; a bonus, as it were—neither the result of training nor experience, but unnatural phenomena. They may be few, but their vocation has a validity which in no way infringes the principle of the corporate character of preaching. In fact, they reinforce it.

For if you lack such special gifts, then better the onus for your stumbling, stuttering, halting speech should be laid upon the Church as a whole than on your personal inadequacies. God can and has used 'men of stammering speech to save his people'.[2]

[2] Isaiah 28:11

FOUR

The Word—Relevant yet Divisive

1 *The Relevant Word*

No issue so torments the mind and conscience of a preacher as the question of relevancy. Congregations demand it— and are often up in arms if they get it—newspaper editors seek it in the form of topical quotes, professors of theology tend to scorn it. But what is *it*?

At first sight, this is a question with an answer so obvious any idiot could expound it at tedious length, and some idiots do. Relevance is the preacher addressing himself to the issues of the day, is it not? Well, yes and no, with reservations on both sides. The search for relevance sorts out the men from the boys, or rather the old from the young, or even more strictly, the Trad from the Trendy.

The preacher who tries to make his sermon 'relevant' evokes from the more starchy members of his congregation the charge that he is always going on about politics. If, on the other hand, he plays for safety and discourses on some fascinating second-century heresies, the young snort with disgust and complain the preacher is not in the real world. A treasured snippet of homiletical lore is the story of the young Oxford curate who transfixed his congregation of farm labourers and chambermaids with the rhetorical question, 'Some of you are probably saying, "So much for Cyril of Jerusalem, but what about Theodore of Mopsuestria?" ' Truly, a son of Sirah who could never be accused of talking down to his congregation—assuming he had one the following week!

Possibly a good pragmatic definition of 'relevance' is the preacher in a situation where he cannot win; in which he balances newspaper against Bible and in his unregenerate moments wishes he could burn both. 'Relevance' has the preacher searching his concordance for a text from which to hang a sermon on the state of the Economy, the evils of Bi-metallism, or the future of the Common Market, not to mention God's solution to the problems of town planning in Sodom and Gomorrah.

Leaving parody aside, the problem of relevant preaching encompasses a veritable minefield of explosive issues which, under certain circumstances, will not only blow the preacher sky-high but also sink his congregation without trace, unless he meets the odd one or two defectors on their way to some neighbouring church where they can be sure of receiving the pure milk of the Gospel, suitably pasteurised and guaranteed free from worldly contamination. And having raised his hat to them, what can he say, other than to echo Jesus' words to his disciples in Gethsemane, 'Sleep on!'?

We are dealing here not solely with what fifty years ago would have been described as the Social Gospel, but with a series of perplexing truths which embody both paradox and contradiction. For instance: how can a preacher be anything other than relevant in the sense of relating to a particular time and place? Biological accident or historical contingency has fixed him, like a fly in amber, in the present and cut him off from both past and future. He cannot be Man in the abstract; only a man of his time. Let him dress, if he will, like Paul or speak the English of Cranmer or profess the faith of a Calvin, Luther or Wesley, but his genetical time-clock can neither be slowed down nor advanced. It will locate him unerringly in the Here and Now. If it doesn't, then a spell in a mental hospital is indicated.

Our faith may have its source in someone who lived two thousand years ago, but we cannot bridge that historical gap and reproduce the circumstances of his life. We cannot return to the New Testament Church, its life-style or thought forms. For we cannot recreate the cultural conditions, the political system, the world-view out of which it sprang and to which it related. Those who regard the present with distaste and attempt to model their common life on that of the primitive Church, end up in some remote valley or clinging to a mountain top striving to hold off the encroachment of the twentieth century. They desire purity and end up cranky. Spiritual Luddites seek to achieve a psychological absurdity—use twentieth-century minds to think first-century thoughts. They have more chance of climbing back into their mothers' womb.

This is the relevance we cannot avoid. 'What I live by,' said Augustine, 'I impart.' That is not a pious hope but an indubitable fact. We can only impart the faith of a Church whose twenty centuries of history are as much a part of it as its present condition. There is no rubbing clean the slate and beginning again. Peel an onion layer by layer and you will not finally uncover an irreducible core. You will be left with an unholy mess—and no onion. So it is with the Church, and the point must be stressed because there are both radical and evangelical factions within it whose zeal has overwhelmed their historical sense as they seek a new beginning, a fresh epiphany of Christ. They wish to remove by some psychic surgery the wrinkles from the face of Mother Church and smooth her gnarled hands.

Such motives are laudable but fundamentally mistaken. Every line on the face of Mother Church is a mark of suffering, just as her roughened hands are the price of servanthood. They are not blemishes but credentials, outward and visible signs of an inward and spiritual wisdom. The Church has *lived*. There is nothing she has not seen and precious few things she has not experienced. Civilizations have crashed about her whilst war and persecution have almost bled her to death; she has lain at ease in Zion and awakened just in time to prevent comfort becoming catalepsy. She has survived many a family feud, her sons in contention with one another to the death.

If it is accepted that the Christian is denied the luxury of plugging in, as it were, to his favourite period of Church history and ignoring all that has happened before or since, then it is clear that he has no option but to relate to his own time and no other. Certainly he is not denied the breadth of vision and depth of understanding which come from inheriting the riches of a comprehensive Christian tradition. We must enter into Life, as John's Gospel would put it, at the precise point where the pressures of history drive its stream past our door.

Wherein, then, lies the problem of relevancy if the preacher has no choice in the matter but to relate to a particular time in a particular place? To begin with, there is a conflict of expectation between what the world asks and the Christian can responsibly deliver. There is a strange idea abroad which Christians who delight in social criticism have done much to foster, that Christianity has something to say about *everything*. In my view, one of the curses of our time is what I would term Conjunctional Christianity. It betrays itself in the title of a thousand books and the theme of numberless conferences—'Christianity *And* . . .'— Christianity and Communism, Christianity and Economic Problems, Christianity and Racism, Christianity and Vegetarianism, Christianity and the Challenge of the Cleckheaton Clog-dancers. Both fundamentalists and liberals are equally disposed to suffer from the malady. The former treat the Bible as a universal encyclopedia of spiritual knowledge—name your problem and pious pundits will fire off a string of texts which purport to offer an inerrant solution to it. The latter believe the Christian Faith can be dissolved without remainder into social issues; that it is a sacred ideology rather than a secular Gospel.

Without doubt, Christians have both the right and duty to comment on contemporary matters, and they may well bring to bear upon them an understanding of Man and the nature of history which adds an extra dimension to their critique. But generally, the Christian thing to say is the sensible thing, neither more nor less.

Pulpit relevance is of a different order from Christian commentary. Ironically, it is based on theological reductionism rather than ethical expansiveness. The preacher recognizes that the greater danger lurks in saying too much rather than too little, in using a shot-gun to pepper with pellets every target in sight instead of the sniper's rifle which scores a single bull. It was no pulpit hack but a theologian as weighty as P. T. Forsyth who said we need less *creed* and more *faith*; that we must reduce the burden of belief upon men because the old orthodoxy bore down upon them with unbearable weight. And, of course, he is right. For who can make all the truths of the Athanasian Creed his own truth every moment of every day?

So relevant preaching has its starting point not in a contemporary issue which preoccupies the congregation's mind but in the historical Gospel reduced to proportions their souls can bear. By all means, the preacher must associate himself with the Church's affirmation of the plenitude of the Christian revelation. If he is wise he will confess the Church's faith is much greater than his own, and if he is shrewd, he will also not expect the world to meet him more than half-way in testing his personal beliefs. Why should it?

He is only one amongst many salesmen competing for its custom. By all means let his meat be strong but if it is so tough as to be indigestible then the public will move on to places where the fare can be swallowed without dyspepsia.

Let there be no misunderstanding. I am not pleading for a painless Gospel—how could I when a Cross is at its focal point?—nor for a bland theology which demands little by way of mental effort or spiritual struggle. The core of relevant preaching is a Gospel which is simple without being simplistic, lean but not anaemic, pared-down yet still whole. Why does relevant preaching demand a minimal theology? After all, our society becomes ever more complex, spawning specialisms with their private language and complicated ideas. The short answer is surely that Christianity came into being out of God's concern to bring his truth within range of the ordinary person. The Incarnation was an exercise in cosmic simplification or it was nothing.

Relevant preaching, then, is made possible by an Incarnational Faith. It is not what the world demands but what God permits that is its rationale. And though, as the cliché has it, the world writes the agenda, it does not also determine the nature of the business. Put differently: relevance means the preacher confronting the world, not trying to lead it or merely echoing it. As in Salvador Dali's striking picture of the Crucifixion, painted from the perspective of the Man on the Cross, the Church's Lord looks down upon the world, not in condescension or contempt, nor yet in detachment— for is not the foot of the Cross embedded in the earth?— but from a situation of agonizing independence. Jesus, of course, described it as being *in* the world but not *of* the world.

Here is a genuine paradox. Whenever we seek to demonstrate the topicality of Christianity, we come up sharply against what might be termed the grand irrelevancy of preaching, the sacrifice of immediate application for ultimate relationship. In all worldly transactions, the preacher represents God's interest, and because God thinks large thoughts and operates according to a time-scale which dwarfs human chronology—'a thousand Ages in thy sight are as an evening gone'—his truths are not Divine solutions to human problems. The opposite is the case. Current issues are parables of his truths or the consequence of defiance of them.

The preacher is not an analyst of economic, social and political problems. Not in his role as *preacher* at any rate. If he has the necessary expertise, he may indeed propose resolutions in ecclesiastical assemblies or write books which expose the ethical implications of technical matters. But as a preacher he must start from the premise that neither Man nor society can be saved by analysis, be it never so profound, but only by a Gospel of Redemption which has its source in the Being of God.

Theological considerations apart, the mechanics of preaching do not lend themselves to contemporary commentary—World Inflation banished in twenty minutes? The Middle East conflict resolved between Introit and Grace? One cannot spell out the totality of the Gospel in that time, let alone deal with all the ramifications of a complex political or economic problem. He who aims at nothing in particular is sure to hit it. To plaster one of the world's running sores with a poultice of generalized clichés is hardly likely to prove the efficacy of the healing Gospel. What, then is the preacher to do—content himself with reciting the Apostle's Creed or Lord's Prayer because both can be guaranteed timeless and comprehensive? There are situations in which he could do much worse. But two points are worth making.

Firstly, Christian truth is indivisible—the whole Gospel is contained in a treatment of any one theme of it. Take, for instance, the highest exercise of Christian love—the forgiveness of our enemies. Not only is the whole of the Christian

Faith implicit in that command of Jesus—Creation, Redemption, Resurrection and Judgement—but equally there are both politically redemptive and economic possibilities in our exercising a degree of forbearance towards those who wish us harm. Providing the core of the doctrine is exposed in a context which gives proper attention to the least used word in the preacher's vocabulary—'How?'—the congregation can make the necessary connection with their own life-situations. Indeed, only in this way can the preacher address 'all sorts and conditions of men'. No twenty-minute excursus can adequately deal with the needs and sins of a hundred or more individuals drawn from many walks of life. Each must be brought face to face with God and made aware of his demands. But they must make their own peace with him. No preacher can stand proxy for them. Nor should he. It is his duty to make the truth plain. By granting men free will, God gives maximum scope for human creativity and imaginativeness in responding to his truth.

Secondly, the preacher cannot do better than study the methods of Jesus. He did not spell out everything in every single pronouncement. But the whole Gospel was implicit in sayings and stories that had a specific and practical point. The motive of his parables was not to cast around the world and find in some life-situation a hidden truth about God, but the precise opposite. He encouraged his hearers to see a bit of human experience through the eyes of God, as it were. Equally, when he was dealing with what we would today regard as a topical issue, he did not embark upon an exhaustive analysis of its various parts. Rather he cut to its heart with a telling phrase, a short story, a touch of irony, a tinge of satire. Above all, he was an affectionate social critic. Even when he was sternly condemning a state of affairs which was an affront to both God and Man, he still found it possible to love those who were perpetuating it.

To do this sort of thing requires hard-won skills—

imagination, sensitivity and, above all, a compassionate understanding of the frailties which drive men to do evil. Such qualities are not acquired by reading text-books about preaching. They are the fruit of a blade-true character allied to absolute confidence in God's mercy and personal experience of his grace—that, plus a keen eye and the self-discipline needed to say too little rather than too much. Which, I suppose, is what Paul meant when he talked about the Spirit testifying to our spirits that we are the children of God. This is the implicit Gospel which strikes home when we have the courage to make explicit the heart of a single aspect of it and leave the rest to God.

Returning to an earlier point. The preacher cannot avoid being relevant in the sense that he must relate to a particular place and time. But he will soon become 'dated' unless he takes seriously the grand irrelevance of preaching and speaks of truths which outlive the flux of time because they issue from the Being of God. Only in this way can the preacher hope to emulate Jesus who, though a man of his time, based his life upon certitudes which relate to the perpetual human condition. None of his values and principles were anchored to the *orbis terrarum*. In their scope and vision they soared beyond the limits of topicality, though they touched down in every time and challenged men to see their actions within a much wider moral context than the standards of the day.

Is not this why Christians for two thousand years have said of Jesus, 'This man is talking to me and my time'? How very different were the worlds of Paul, Augustine, Aquinas, Luther, Wesley, William Booth and Pope John! Yet each knew that a word spoken in first-century Palestine was addressed personally to them. That is the difference between relevance and topicality. A topical word loses its meaning when the time to which it was addressed gives place to another. A relevant word is intelligible in every time because it is the earthly echo of the voice of the Lord of all history.

2 *The Divisive Word*

We talk of the Gospel as Good News. But, in fact, the Gospel is Bad News for some because it strikes at the heart of human egotism and selfishness. Jesus recognized this when he claimed to have come to bring not peace but a sword, which would cut the ties of kinship—setting father against son, mother against daughter. And so it was. One has only to read between the lines in Paul's Letters to realize the uproar, even chaos, created by the Gospel amongst Jewish Christians and the first generation of Gentile converts. Families were split, friendships sundered, communities divided. Nor was the conflict confined to Jews versus Christians or Christians versus the devotees of the Mystery Religions. Primitive Christianity polarized around its charismatic leaders. The disciples of Paul were at odds with those of Peter or James or Apollos. It is some reassurance to modern Christians struggling to unite the various Denominations, that the early Church also suffered from divisiveness—and survived!

The essence of the problem is not human frailty but the nature of the Gospel itself. For it offers both comfort and challenge. It comforts the distressed but equally tends to distress the comfortable with its insistence that they ought not to avert their gaze from the poor, disadvantaged and oppressed. And which decent, reasonably well-blessed citizen, honest to a fault and philanthropic to the degree his circumstances will allow, reacts favourably to the announcement that his righteousness is as filthy rags in the sight of God?

Not without anguish, tears and anger was the New Testament written; not without anguish, tears and anger can it be received as Gospel. There is a radical discontinuity between conventional morality and Christian obedience.

Hence, the mystery is not that the Gospel is divisive but why it so rarely divides the average congregation.

Sheer repetition has much to do with it. The cutting edge of the Gospel has been blunted by easy familiarity. Traditional churchgoers are word-perfect on whole passages of the Sermon on the Mount or some of Paul's most scarifying anathemas. It is their memories rather than their consciences which are taxed when they are called upon to say together the General Confession or respond to the liturgical recital of the Commandments of our Lord. It is like swallowing an oyster or wearing an old slipper—no astringency nor angularities.

The preacher has the perennial task of trying to prevent truth whose rough edges have been rubbed smooth through constant usage from sliding straight into the hearer's unconscious without ever demanding his conscious attention. A congregation's reaction to a Bible reading couched in the majestic if opaque language of the Authorized Version compared to the same theme spelled out during the sermon demonstrates the point. They will accept from Isaiah a lambasting in Gothic English with something akin to complacency, but let the preacher express the same sentiments in the language of the *Daily Mirror* and they will be baying for his blood!

Rhythm not only rocks a baby to sleep but equally anaesthetizes a congregation. The lilting cadences of archaic or even formal English robs sense of its sting. The hymn writer can compose his stanzas warning of the Dreadful Day of the Lord when miserable sinners such as we will suffer unspeakable torment, yet provided preacher or organist mates the words to a good rousing tune, the congregation will bellow their imminent doom with gusto, eyes bright and feet tapping. I once heard an eminent theologian who, when asked if he could say the Apostle's Creed with absolute conviction, replied, 'No, but I can sing it!'

A note of caution must be sounded at this point. One can understand the exasperation of the preacher whose congregation treats his lion-like roars as though they were the mewings of a kitten. But he must resist the temptation to shock them into attention out of the mistaken idea that there is therapeutic value in a swift kick in the pants for its own sake. The scandal of the Gospel is inherent within it and not to be added as an optional extra by pulpit pyrotechnics. By all means stab a congregation awake so long as the process stops short of hacking them to death.

I have witnessed one of America's best known radicals so bent on cracking the crustacean complacency of a middle-class congregation that he lit a cigarette in the pulpit and peppered his sermon with four-letter words. The tragedy was that he roused them neither to contrition nor Christian action but to righteous indignation. As a result they were deaf to what he was actually saying—which was a powerful exposition of the Gospel. He took an almost gleeful pride in the fact that no congregation ever invited him to preach to them twice. But he would not accept that there is an eternity of difference between the moral offence of the Gospel and the gratuitous offensiveness of one who purports to preach it.

Admittedly, this was an extreme case, but it offers a salutary warning against mistaking courage for braggadocio, good technique with bad manners. The preacher may have to contend with his congregation but he must not show contempt for them. It is a besetting sin of the radical (and I count myself as one) that he tends to cherish the world like a mistress and treats the Church less as a mother than a stage mother-in-law, to be dragged about the place by the hair. There is something plain contrary about being concerned to offer redemption to a world that does not want it whilst denying it to the Church which, for all its faults, is praying for it.

But the divisiveness of the Gospel is not a consequence of the idiosyncracies of any particular preacher. It separates those who will hear its discordant alarm from those who wish to sleep on. We are prone to stand the truth on its head and claim that life is ridden with conflict which the Gospel subdues into harmony. In fact, it is the Gospel which injects the conflict into our peaceful lives, shattering the pact of mutual non-aggression we have concluded with God, our society and our inner selves. He who looks to Jesus for a way *out* of his troubles will be abashed to find he is offered instead a way *through* them—a much more rigorous remedy than he had bargained for. And we can hardly say we have not been warned, for as Mark Twain is reputed to have commented, what is so troubling about the Gospel is not the part we fail to understand but what we understand quite clearly and cannot stomach.

So the preacher confronts his people not as an insurance salesman; more like a recruiting sergeant—what is on offer is not an all-risks policy but the King's Shilling; not peace but a sword. Like Jesus, according to the writer of *Hebrews*, we learn obedience by the things we suffer. If the Gospel backs us up at all, it backs us up into a corner; increasing our anxiety not abating it; not resolving our problems but adding to them. There has to be a rooting out before there can be a planting, a shaking of the foundations before anything of lasting worth can be built. Preaching is, in the words of Paul Scherer, a thoroughly radical transaction, getting right down to the roots of our dilemma, acting more like a dentist's drill than a good dose of aspirin.

Mother Church betrays all the symptoms of self-indulgence—flaccid, neurotic, over-nourished and under-exercised. She is paying the price for a period in which preaching degenerated into a vapid moralizing, vividly characterized in Richard Niebhur's epigram as testifying to a God without wrath, who brings men without sin, into a Kingdom without

Judgement through a Christ without a Cross. And what is divisive about that pseudo-gospel? We can all accept it without pain. Like all placebos, it will not heal us but can be guaranteed to cause us no discomfort.

Forty years ago, Dr H. H. Farmer diagnosed the malaise of preaching as making claims too small, too confident, and too easy to be true. I would add a fourth—too generalized to be true. The Gospel does not cover the universal human condition, which is sordid, messy and dishevelled, with a pink mist of spirituality. Instead, it acts upon the pressure-points of individual lives, challenging attitudes to matters so down to earth as sex, ambition, power, race and money. All Christians might agree that God is love, sin is bad and Jesus is the Greatest. But put the knife in and jab the nerve that connects with their political opinions, economic prospects and social situation and expect an almighty yell, not to mention a rare old barney, with one lot against the other and both against you. And yet that is precisely where the knife must go because, Damascus Road experiences excepted, men are not converted in the twinkling of an eye but bit by bit, habit by habit, attitude by attitude. Didn't Jesus say that where our treasure is, there will our heart be also? Presumably he countenanced a conversion at the level of our pockets which in due time might extend to the rest of us.

Preaching brought to a burning focus upon the pressure points of personality is bound to be divisive. For it to be anything else is a crass betrayal of the Gospel. In most human situations there is that 'one thing needful' which cuts to the heart of some characteristic sin of a particular generation, class or racial group. It won't be their only sin but it will be symptomatic of the rest as a white spot betrays a leper. Medieval preachers gave pre-eminence in the demonic league table to Pride. A quick sweep of the history of the first half of the twentieth century suggests that Cruelty

has relegated Pride to second place. I would rate Discrimination in all its forms as the characteristic sin of our time,
allowing that it contains elements of both pride and cruelty
within it.

Here then is the nub of the paradox which holds together
preaching that is both relevant and divisive. Relevance
demands that the preacher sacrifice immediate application
for fundamental certitudes which soar beyond the limits of
topicality and yet touch down in every time and situation;
at the same time the Gospel is bound to be divisive because
it homes in upon a specific sin, inevitably stirring up controversy because it takes an axe to the tree under which we
shelter, coddling our pet foibles, so pathetically human but
potentially deadly.

Let me take refuge from theorizing in personal experience.
I know what I know, not because I have mastered the Art
of the Sermon, but because I am still nursing the wounds
sustained in the course of discovering just how divisive the
Gospel can be. Like the little man who leaned against the
wall of a skyscraper and was aghast when the whole building
fell on him, I entered a situation of racial tension and
preached the odd sermon about human equality and the
God-given dignity of all men. They were not particularly
good sermons, but before I knew it my congregation was
in uproar, my church desecrated and my manse under siege.

From the convalescent home, as it were, I offer a few
practical hints to anyone who feels constrained to apply the
sharp end of the Gospel to a tender area of social tissue
whether in his own community or elsewhere.

Firstly, the preacher must beware of becoming a one-
string fiddle, harping monotonously upon a single issue,
however urgent or contentious it may be. It is the fullness
of the Gospel which has converting power, not any particular theme isolated from the rest. The biggest bores in
Christendom are those utterly committed preachers who,

whatever the occasion or Season of the Christian Year, manage to gallop into church on their favourite hobby-horse and do not dismount until they have ridden it to death. Their ingenuity is commendable, but their churchmanship is appalling. The Gospel is not synonymous with Pacifism, Socialism, Racial Equality or whatever. The congregation is not a pressure group, to be recruited to a social crusade. The Kingly Rule of God is not to be equated with an end to war, the dawning of world socialism, or the abandonment of all discrimination. It may embrace all three but it is neither defined nor exhausted by them. Nor must it be assumed that those Christians who are not of the preacher's own persuasion are *ipso facto* doomed to Outer Darkness from which they may eventually, through the mercy of God, arrive at the gates of the Kingdom by a round about way.

Indeed, I would claim that the plenitude of the Gospel, far from being the opiate of the people, reinforces the stand on a single issue the preacher feels impelled to make. A congregation quickly becomes inoculated against pulpit perorations which blast away at a single target week after week. The preacher thinks he is putting his hearers under Judgement; in fact, the only judgement they are likely to make is that he is not so much a prophet as an eccentric. And should they take themselves off to some other church where they have an even chance of hearing the full orchestration of the Christian message rather than a one-note sonata for solo violin, it is dangerous for the preacher to derive a perverted pride from his empty pews—as though they are a testimony to his outspokenness. They may be more a symptom of theological imbalance.

Take the issue of Race which activates the deepest prejudices of many otherwise decent people. During my first months in Africa I attempted to get some of my White congregation to change their attitudes and abandon the colour bar they had been maintaining in the nicest possible way from time immemorial. I preached sermon after sermon seeking to demonstrate Black equality on anthropological, ethical, political and historical grounds. The response was nil. If anything I was strengthening defences I sought to demolish. I finally realized that it was a case of the semi-literate preaching to the half-converted—*I* was not deploying the total resources of the Gospel; *they* were just not Christian at the level of their racial attitudes. What was required was not so much advocacy as evangelism. The theme of racial justice is not an ethical outworking of the Gospel; rather, it is inherent in the whole Gospel of Creation, Redemption and Judgement. The racists in my congregation did not need convincing; they needed converting. It was Jesus through their Black neighbour with whom they had first to come to terms.

It would be idle to pretend that the Gospel did painlessly what my perfervid oratory failed to achieve. I lost a number of church members, but those who remained had a decisive effect on the character of a whole community.

This leads naturally to my second piece of gratuitous advice. When dealing with contentious issues, the preacher must, to use an idiom from a very different field, throw the Book at his congregation! This is just a fancy way of saying that his theme ought not only to flow from the words of Scripture in the form of a text but also be based upon an intelligent and judicious exposition of it. It is good Protestant teaching that the Bible is the only rule of faith and practice, but we do well to remember that there is only such a rule because God rules. Hence, God's Word is dynamic. It is as contemporary as God himself. The rule of Scripture cannot be the crude and dead literalism that certain parts of the Dutch Reformed Church apply in order to reinforce their perverted racial attitudes. As Luther constantly reminded us, Christ is the judge of Scripture, and the written word must be weighed by its testimony to the living Word. The preacher misuses the Bible when he searches its pages for some ingenious text which can be developed to give authority to his views, be they never so sound.

I am not arguing that every sermon should be expository in style. But I would submit that where the matters dealt with are likely to be highly controversial and strike at the deepest held convictions of a congregation, the preacher should ensure that his treatment is Biblically sound; and this, for two reasons. Firstly, Scripture has an authority to which he cannot aspire, however brilliant or gifted he may be. Secondly, when a congregation is likely to be resistant to what the preacher says, it is infinitely preferable that those who fight the truth hardest should be forced to argue with the Bible rather than with the occupant of the pulpit. Should any be so outraged as to quit the church, then it must be obvious to those who remain that defectors have not been driven out but have rejected the claims of the Gospel.

A final point which has more to do with good manners than sound theology. Unless specifically requested to do so, no preacher ought to proclaim the Gospel at its most divisive to a congregation other than his own. It requires little heroism to set off a bomb and then dash for home, leaving the resident minister to deal with the resulting uproar. It is a corollary of the divisiveness of the Gospel that a preacher only has the right to expound it from his pulpit provided he is prepared to defend it afterwards in his people's homes, and also exercise a pastoral ministry to those who may find the attitudes and habits of a life-time threatened. Not only knaves resist the Gospel. All of us do to some degree. Therefore let the minister who is a lion in the pulpit be a diligent shepherd out of it, doing everything possible, within the limits of his integrity, to enable as many of his critics as will open their door to him to state their views and voice their doubts.

But when every qualification has been stated and every allowance made for the frailty of human nature, the preacher must stand firm upon the Gospel, 'whether the people will hear or whether they will forbear', for it is not his integrity but that of God's Word which is at stake. To speak a relevant yet divisive word is often to embark upon a lonely and sometimes even dangerous road. No one in his right mind goes out of his way to cultivate unpopularity. No one in his right mind can view with equanimity the shattering of Christian fellowship and the Church in uproar. When a preacher's congregation shrinks and he is overwhelmed by a sense of failure, it is well he should remember that God plus one is a majority—which is unlikely to console him but might at least nerve him to continue the task to which he has set his hand.

FIVE

The Word—Prophetic yet Priestly

THERE is an apparent contradiction between the preacher's twin roles as prophet and priest. And I use the term 'priest' not in its technical vocational sense to describe a parson professing a particular brand of churchmanship, but functionally in a way which could apply equally to minister or layman. Nor am I thinking of the clash between the prophets and priests within the Church. That is a squabble with an honorable ancestry stretching back to Moses and Aaron. I am more concerned with the interior tension between prophet and priest in every preacher.

The preacher is servant of a historical word in the sense that it refers to unrepeatable events encompassing a life and work—that of Jesus—which is complete and sealed. It is a priestly role to preserve the record of these events and rehearse them within the Church for ever. But this word is also an apostolic word which needs new voices and accents to tell it forth in every time as God's response to contemporary happenings. That is a prophetic function.

Priestly obedience is to a tradition which enshrines what God has done, a distinctive testimony for the ages. Prophetic obedience is to a vision—God's Being reflected in the events of a particular time. The preacher as prophet has a clear duty to urge the people forward into the unknown, confident that God has gone ahead. The preacher as priest has an equally plain duty to preserve the people from taking an irretrievable step into apostasy. The priest names the name of Jesus who is for ever the Christ, Lord and Saviour. The prophet takes his stand by the Jesus who is known within history by many names or none.

Of course, I am overstating the distinction between the preacher's prophetic and priestly functions in order to sharpen the argument. But if the tension between prophet and priest was acute in Biblical times, how much more agonising can it become in the modern church, where the preacher must discharge both roles?

Granted, there are certain areas where there need be no conflict between prophetic and priestly obedience. They can, in fact, be harmonized—in the renewed emphasis upon the unity of worship and mission or that sacramental theology which is based upon the idea of the prophetic breaking in of the world upon the very centre of what used to be thought of as the most priestly of rites.

But there *are* points of conflict, and the attempt to do justice to both his priestly and prophetic roles can tear a preacher apart. Let the word from the pulpit strike at the nub of a highly contentious issue and the prophetic thrust may undercut the preacher's priestly authority. Congregations do not find it easy to receive comfort and challenge from the same source. Pierce their ear-drums with your prophetic thunderings and you often render them deaf to your priestly admonition.

Undoubtedly, for many reasons, a preacher will put more emphasis on either priestly or prophetic elements in his vocation, but at all costs he must not cut the gordian knot and become either prophet or priest. For he can only speak a truly contemporaneous, prophetic word when the full burden of the historic truth of the Gospel has rested upon him, otherwise he degenerates into a commentator on

74

current affairs. And from being a priest he will become an antiquarian unless that Faith once delivered to the saints, of which he is a guardian, is constantly exposed to the gospel the world preaches to the Church.

So let us look in turn at the prophetic and priestly words which are held in tension within the Word, taking note that it is only for convenience they *can* be separated. In the person of the preacher they constitute an unresolvable paradox with which he must live as best he may.

1 *The Prophetic Word*

The Church has its 'in-words'—dialogue, involvement, ecumenicity. At the present time the supreme compliment it can pay one of its preachers is to attach the adjective 'prophetic' to his name. Then he becomes the darling of the theological students and the bane of their teachers. His lightest word is treated as holy writ, and the adulation he receives from radicals is only exceeded by the degree of suspicion he arouses in religious Establishments.

There *are* men and women in the modern Church who are worthy to be named in the same breath as those wild men of the Old Testament, but they are in such short supply that some churchmen take the Pauline view that the pro-phetic office is a form of specialism—'He called some to be apostles, some prophets, some evangelists, some pastors and teachers. . . .' There is however, I would submit, New Testament warrant for rejecting the view that prophets are a sort of crack corps in the army of the Lord. That wry wish of Moses, recorded in *Numbers,* 'Would that *all* the Lord's people were prophets!' was granted a long time later at Pentecost where '*All* present were filled with the Spirit and began to speak . . .'. From that time on, prophecy ceases to be the monopoly of the favoured few and becomes an essential dimension in the witness of every preacher.

Which is all very well, but how does the preacher *do* it? What does it mean to be prophetic in our own little patch? I have found that the most effective way of getting at an answer to this crucial question is by pointing out the differences between true and false prophets.

(i) False prophets look to the Bible for answers: true prophets allow it to pose the questions.

It is hard to convince many Christians that the Bible is not a time-capsule preprogrammed by God a long time ago to bellow forth at the touch of a button infallible answers to any problem history can throw up. With breathtaking gall, we tap on the shoulder men of affairs wrestling with complex issues which baffle the best minds of our day and assure them that the answers they seek are to be found in the Ten Commandments or the Sermon on the Mount or wherever.

This slab of history with the roof off we call the Bible; this record of the totality of a people's life lived out in the presence of God is not primarily designed to offer inerrant solutions to historical problems. What it does is to pose inescapable questions which men of this or any age attempt to evade at their peril, and it is these questions which are the touchstone of its relevance and contemporaneity:

God to Adam: 'Where art thou?'

Isaiah to the People of Israel: 'Why will this nation perish for disobeying God?'

Jesus to every Christian: 'Why do you call me Lord and ignore the things I command you?'

Paul and Barnabus to the people of Lystria: 'Why do you put your trust in gods that cannot save?'

Such formal questions (and according to my concordance, allowing for variants of the same incident, Jesus began no less than 150 sentences with the word 'Why') together with the questions raised by our general reading of the Bible have special significance because they demand personal responses

76

not academic answers. God's questions to men issue in costly action rather than interesting discussion.

God's Word is in the questions because he treats us as human beings, giving scope for creativity in seeking the answers. He does not reduce us to the status of mindless megaphones, passing on to our fellowmen messages broadcast from a transmitting station beyond the stars and reduced to written form by courtesy of the British and Foreign Bible Society.

Permit me a degree of over-simplification in developing this argument. Of course there *are* commandments in the Bible which enjoin our obedience. They usually relate to the fundamental conversion situation, God confronting Man with an intolerable yet inevitable demand. The ultimate religious question was put to God by Paul on the Damascus road, 'Lord, what wilt thou have me to do?' The man who asks *that* question will undoubtedly get an answer. He may not like it, but he'll get it! Yet except for these most intimate transactions between the fugitive human soul and a pursuing God, nothing else in the Bible is cut and dried. No prepacked Divine solutions to the dilemmas of Christian discipleship are likely to drop into our laps.

It is interesting that the Austrian psychiatrist, Victor Frankl, makes a similar point from his own experience which included a spell in a Nazi death camp: 'We need to stop asking about the meaning of life and instead think of ourselves as those who are questioned by life. . . .' He goes on to quote Nietzsche: 'He who has a why to live for can bear almost any how.'[1]

A practical example is better than any amount of theorizing. Take the issue of violence as a solution to the problem of justice. If we go to the Bible seeking some resolution of the grievous dilemma expressed in the relationship between love and power, we end up, pacifist versus non-pacifist,

[1] Quoted by Paul Scherer, *The Word God Sent*, p. 100 (Hodder, 1966)

standing eyeball-to-eyeball, hitting one another over the head with Biblical texts which seem to support our case. The result is what I believe is called a Mexican Stand-Off. If however we steep ourselves in the questions raised by the history of God's Israel and in the totality of the Jesus-Event, it may be possible for both pacifists and non-pacifists to make creative responses to those questions without either one denying the light by which the other walks.

To put the issue baldly: the false prophet says that life raises questions to which the Bible supplies answers; the true prophet looks for creative responses in his own life and the life of society to the questions the Bible poses.

(ii) The false prophet is a moralist—he tells the world how things ought to be; the true prophet is a realist—he tells the world how things really are.

It is interesting to conjecture why the Bible has remained comparatively uncensored. Why was it not cleaned up before publication like the parliamentary record in those countries where politicians are allowed to erase their more asinine remarks before they come to the public's attention? There is a rigorous honesty about the Bible which is breathtaking. As the Yanks would say, it tells it like it is, not the way we or anyone else would like it to be. So the crude, blood-stained bits have been left in; the arrant paganism; the flirting with false gods; those bursts of hatred that almost curl the edges of the paper.

The Bible tells it like it is because the truth is redemptive. Before World War I, Woodrow Wilson said this: 'The new radicalism (in politics) will consist not in the things proposed but in the things disclosed.' A better definition of prophecy it would be hard to find. The prophet is not a moralist, dreaming of some antiseptic Utopia where men do as they ought; he is a realist, uncovering the truth about the world as it really is.

A determination to tell it the way it is cannot be too highly prized in a society adept at self-delusion; which puts unpleasant things in fancy wrappings and gives pretty names to ugly realities. We talk about aid when we mean fraud; development when we have exploitation in mind; we propose charity when we ought to be making reparation.

A whole new industry has grown up dedicated to providing those who can pay for the service with a 'good' image, and these professional whitewash merchants have enough skill to project the Dick Turpins of public life as though they were the Good Samaritan. There are advertising agencies who can doctor manure so that it tastes like caviar and smells of *eau de cologne* and then convince the public that no home is complete without the delicacy.

Whenever men say one thing and mean another; wherever they try to oversimplify complex issues or make simple issues complex; when they are apt to delude themselves or seek to delude others, there is a crying need for prophets who will tell it like it is—get beneath the rationalization and verbiage in order to uncover the truth. Never mind proposing fancy programmes in terms of what ought to be in the best of all possible worlds. The prophetic task is to get at the truth about this world, believing that every testimony to the truth is an affirmation of the one who is the Truth. For however pleasant or sordid, hard or easy the reality of any situation may be, the truth by its nature is redemptive and creative; it both judges and heals. And furthermore it is a prophetic conviction that once the truth is known, injustice cannot long prevail, at least not without revealing its ugly face. Isn't this what Jesus meant when he talked of the truth making us free?

We have got to tell it the way it is because we believe that Divinity is not remote in the ultimate Why of things—that is the God of the metaphysicians—but close at hand in the immediate How of things—the God of the prophets.

(iii) False prophets speak a simple word of Promise or Judgement; true prophets speak a paradoxical word of Promise and Judgement.

When the Hebrew prophets tried to puzzle out what God was saying to their nation, they discovered a strange thing about his mode of address. He always spoke a word of promise which offered fulfilment and a satisfying destiny, but if the people seized the promise and forgot the terms on which it was offered, that same word was transformed by their disobedience into judgement. Yet even when the faithless nation was carried off captive and suffered a terrible fate at the hands of their enemies, the prophets never lost hope or made the mistake of assuming that God's word of judgement had cancelled out his original promise, or else his ultimate purpose could never be achieved. And so on the far side of tragedy, whilst they still lay deep in judgement, the Jews heard a new promise which gave them a fresh lease of life—'Babylon is fallen!'

So the truly prophetic word has moral depth. It is never flippant or casually simple because it is addressed to Man who oscillates between extremes of pride and humility, misery and grandeur. And this word speaks of promise *and* judgement, because men need both to be jolted into a sense of dignity when they are grovelling in the dust and knocked off their perch when they get cocky and forget that they too are God's creatures.

False prophets, whose interpretation of life is always neat and tidy, will not wrestle with the ambiguities of this paradoxical word and so they tear apart its two halves and become soothsayers of unmitigated doom or purveyors of unalloyed bliss. They speak a word of promise that fills men with unwarranted optimism or a simple word of judgement which drives them to ultimate despair.

Two illustrations make the point. Successive presidents of the United States have proved falsely prophetic about the Vietnam war. They spoke words of promise untempered by judgement, offering confident predictions that victory would be won this year, next year, the year after; exclamations of satisfaction that communism was being contained in South-East Asia and the boys would soon be home. And so unwarranted optimism lured the United States deeper and deeper into a morass from which they almost found it impossible to extricate themselves. Had promise been balanced by judgement, the nation might have been nerved for the moral harrowing it was to undergo, suffering wounds which would bleed not only its manpower but its very soul.

Consider the opposite case. The 'Keep Britain White!' extremists are false prophets because they are offering words of judgement without promise. They are chilling the nation's blood with prognostications about the horrid consequences of continued coloured immigration but never a word about the economic contribution these new citizens might make, let alone the enrichment of our tired, grey, national life by the injection of other cultures.

Jesus must be our model here. All his great promises embodied judgement because each one concluded with an unspoken 'but if not!' And yet his harshest judgements offered men promise for they aimed at bringing them to the point of a contrition which destroyed their pride without extinguishing their hope. This is surely the essence of true prophecy—a word of judgement which leads men to penitence and yet embodies promise, the assurance that forgiveness is possible and available.

So much for the preacher as prophet, but that is only half his role—speaking in God's name to men. He is also called to speak in man's name to God—this is his priestly role, and it allows him no lofty detachment. His voice does not come *to* the Church but rises *from* it. Hence, he is, in this identification with a community of faith which can make no pretensions to infallibility, 'a man of unclean lips who dwells amongst a people of unclean lips'—to quote Isaiah.

Any authentic word he speaks is wrung out of wrestling with the peculiar tensions which stretch on the wrack anyone who dares to handle holy things.

2 *The Priestly Word*

The preacher is a man who deals in power, and the more effective he is, the greater his power, though it is over a particular constituency and is of a special sort. But the Word whose servant he is exposes both the absurdity of success and the dignity of defeat.

We preachers are followers of one who, according to the Bible, was despised and rejected of men, and we have no right to expect any different fate. We fulfil our vocation by sharing the suffering of God. We glory in the uniqueness of a Faith which proclaims that God has put himself at men's mercy and gives them strength through his weakness and power by his impotence. We serve the God who is content to be the anonymous neighbour, having no form nor likeness that we should desire him. We know that we are only vindicated by defeat—the Cross teaches *that* if it teaches anything. But here is the problem. . . .

Our aptitudes and abilities, good in themselves, are God's gift to us. It is a consequence of having been given dominion that what we do we try to do well; having put our hands and heads and hearts to any task, we strive to accomplish it with all our might. Hence, we hope to make a good job of commending our Saviour—to be faithful and powerful servants of the Word. So, absurdity of absurdities, we strain to make a success of proclaiming Divine failure. We wish to excel in the business of pointing men to cosmic defeat.

We are trapped in a vicious circle. Our honest workmanship and legitimate skill in commending the Gospel are taken up by the world, transmuted into its own coinage—from effectiveness to success—and rung up on the cash register of public acclaim. We are inundated with invitations to preach on special occasions. Our diaries, crammed with engagements stretching ahead into the future, are tangible proof of our mastery of the preacher's art. The dilemma is exquisite. The priestly word tends to fill the pews the prophetic word empties. And this, not necessarily because the preacher is ducking any issues and crying 'peace, peace, where there is no peace'. It is his task to build up the Church, to strengthen the faith of the fitfully Faithful, to offer them the succour of the Gospel, to tether them in the stormy seas to the Anchor that cannot be moved—above all, to intercede for them before God. Whereas the prophet wrestles *with* men, the priest wrestles *for* them, and not unnaturally they will love and respect him for it. Yet priests cannot ever be at peace, for they are haunted by the gaunt figure of the one who mocks their modicum of fame by his total obscurity, their eloquence by his silence, their panoply by his nakedness.

Outstanding advocacy of the Gospel will result in lionization, if not from the world then from a religious constituency which delights in its star performers. For in a day when the Church takes many blows, Christians demand their heroes in order to bolster their battered confidence. The slogan of Dr Graham's second Earl's Court Campaign—'Billy's Back!'—was the retort of a hero-starved religious public to the pop-world's triumphant halloo—'The Beatles Are Here!' We too can fill our halls and draw the crowds!

So the priestly word will be muted, not because it is false but because the preacher lives with inner contradictions which only God in his good time can resolve.

But that is by no means the end of the story. If success were the only peril we have to withstand, we might just about cope. But the issue cuts deeper into that hidden dimension of life concerned with power. The handling of power is the inevitable consequence of exercising dominion.

We possess it and we have no option but to use it or be used by it. Power is the ability to accomplish purpose, and little can be done without the application of the appropriate degree of it at the right time. So here we are, proclaiming the powerlessness of God from within that structure of power called the Church. He who does not recognize that there is in the most solemn of religious assemblies an element of power politics at work is not so much pious as naïve. In addition to those venerable categories of apostles, prophets and martyrs, it is time the Church paid liturgical tribute to its 'holy jostle of power politicians' who, by their mastery of men, money and machinery, accomplish much for the Kingdom.

Yet we know full well that power always exacts too high a price for its services. We preachers, being held in an honour we often do not deserve, tend to be the appointed spokesmen for one of the great institutions of our time. Our place in the hierarchy may vary but it is of the nature of the Church that where it exists at all, it exists in its entirety, so the priestly word is always backed by an unstable amalgam of secular and spiritual power. But there is no alternative. In order to be effective witnesses of the powerlessness of God, through which, regardless of the horror of the Jews and the sneers of the Gentiles, the ultimate thing is accomplished, we must touch, handle and risk being totally compromised by power, whether it be that of the village church council or the great Denominational headquarters.

Besides power, the preacher as priest deals in a special kind of knowledge. In particular, he is master of a body of knowledge which provides answers to questions few outside the Church are asking. It is the authority as well as the relevance of the sacred truths of which the preacher is 'professor' that is under question. Theology, once queen of the sciences, is now jostled by all kinds of upstarts in the democracy of intellectual disciplines. She no longer has an *a priori* claim to be heard with respect. Her authority is solely that of the degree of receptivity she calls out in those who are open to her claims. The application of the scientific method to the Biblical corpus has destroyed for all time the mystique, even magic, that once attached to it. The West has its *gurus* all right, but they are to be found in laboratories and not in pulpits.

The preacher as prophet can roam the world, poking his nose where he will, speaking of matters as topical as today's newspaper. The preacher as priest is guardian of a finite body of knowledge whose roots delve deep into history. And it cannot be gainsaid that a fundamentalism of either Bible or Church which makes no attempt to come to terms with God's world except to treat it as a captive audience will indeed render the preacher irrelevant to all except the minority who share his presuppositions. But the priest must not lose his nerve and go to the opposite extreme and succumb to the myth of the world's omnipotence in both asking and answering every question the mind of mortal man can raise. This is to romanticize the secular disciplines and assume that in contrast to the Church's obscurantism, worldly knowledge has a high degree of intelligibility about the issues which really perplex mankind. The present state of society is scarcely a glowing testimony to the ability of the secular Big Brains to come up with practical solutions to Man's basic problems.

The preacher as priest addresses the world obliquely, as it were, through the Church, not in a spirit of empiricism but from the standpoint of biblical faith. And truly sensitive and intelligent biblical interpretation can provide a standing ground detached from technical discussion yet dominating it. I would, however, stress that word 'intelligent'. The use of the Bible as a leather-bound *Old Moore's Almanac* is to be deplored as re-introducing sheer superstition into a world which banished it along with the ducking of witches and the belief that mental disease was evidence of Satanism. True biblical exposition demands a high degree of critical intelligence and theological acumen. Above all, it calls for humility before the truth and the rejection of all claims to priestly infallibility. I would contend that more preachers tender themselves irrelevant through ignorance of the Bible than because of lack of interest in the contents of the daily newspaper.

I would insist that mastery of biblical faith is no ivory-tower exercise remote from wordly involvement. The preacher as priest could not avoid being secular man even if his life depended upon it. He has been granted no God-given immunity from the pressures which are transforming the contemporary world. Indeed, these pressures in the West have either been generated by the Christian Faith or by reaction against it.

Whether the preacher as priest is a religious professional or what is loosely termed a layman there is one thing he must have mastered before he dare set foot in a pulpit. He must know how to lead people to their Lord. The frontiers of religious knowledge are vague and ill-defined, but the centre is fixed. It is the saving truth of Jesus Christ.

Can any preacher ever be prophet and priest at the same time? He has no option, for there are occasions when he is God's sacrament to men, others when he stands for men's sacrifice to God. Through him the human spirit speaks to God and the Holy Spirit speaks to men. The tension is agonizing. After all, it broke Christ's heart. It will certainly rend his own spirit. But it must be done, for the preacher who is prophet but not priest can apply the lash but not bind up the wounds. And the priest who is not prophet may comfort the patient but not cut out his cancer.

So from one voice issue both the prophetic and priestly word. But not, I hasten to add, at the same time, otherwise his congregation will be in total disarray. If he draws his power from the proper source he will be shown when to warn and when to woo; to thunder or to whisper; to build up or cast down. It matters not that he speaks in two tones so long as they are harmonized by a fully orchestrated theology in which every major note of the Christian Faith is regularly sounded.

SIX

The Word—Liturgical and Sacramental

LET me come clean at the outset and confess that I can find
little by way of contrast let alone paradox between the two
halves of this theme. Indeed, far from there being any
tension between the liturgical and sacramental words, one
was at the heart of the other in the Early Church. The people
of God assembled for the primary purpose of breaking
bread together—it was the focal point, the climax of the
ritual. Only after the Reformation did beetle-browed pan-
Protestants, like quartermasters in a fortress under siege by
legions of Rome, severely ration the bread and wine. Once
a month or quarter or even year was considered sufficiently
frequent to celebrate Holy Communion without transforming it into an act of homage to the Harlot of Babylon. They
say the Devil enters the Church through the choir; some of
our fathers were equally sure that the Pope insinuated
himself curled up inside a communion goblet.

Whilst staunchly affirming that liturgy and sacrament
belong together, it seems to me that there are points to be
made about each which justify separate treatment.

1 *The Liturgical Word*

I doubt the word 'liturgism'[1] exists (if it does, it ought not

[1] Used by Helmut Thielicke, *The Trouble with the Church* (Hodder, 1966),
though in a pejorative sense.

to) but the practice assuredly does and it rings as phoney as the term which describes it. It is a luxuriant but poisonous growth which feeds on the decay of preaching. For whatever motives, some preachers convinced that they ought to vacate the pulpit because the sermon is an out-moded form of communication, have taken up new positions at the altar, in the middle of the congregation or even swinging from the chandeliers, and join with gusto in all kinds of sanctified acrobatics, carrying the people, willingly or unwillingly with them. The colours are riotous, the noise deafening and the movement frenzied. The result is a 'happening' which may have a brief vogue until the congregation realize they can enjoy a similar spectacle at the local circus, with performing seals and elephants thrown in.

In case I should be accused of parodying a burgeoning movement of liturgical experiment, I quote the synopsis of an actual service described by John Killinger in his Handbook for Experimental Worship, *Leave it to the Spirit:*

> The congregation enters in absolute silence, and after a few minutes, a man near the front of the congregation stands up and begins to remove his clothes. Someone near him, having been provided with a grease crayon, begins to write aggression or resentment phrases on him. Someone else joins the first writer. They, in turn, pass the crayons on to others and urge them to write on the man.
>
> While the people continue to write upon the first man, a woman in another part of the room rises and begins to disrobe. The same process is followed. Elsewhere, a third person rises and repeats the action; a fourth, a fifth, perhaps more. The ministers who have been robed and seated facing the congregation in the beginning must take part in these rites also.
>
> When the graffitti-bearers are all marked up, they begin to race about the room, crying and screaming, the music becomes tumultuous and cacophonous. Members of the congregation should likewise howl and scream, some might even produce drums and castanets.

During the mêlée, a figure in white robes walks quietly down the centre aisle to the altar and begins to disrobe, laying his clothes aside very carefully. He may be painted as a harlequin, either in every bright splotches of colour or in black and white waves emanating from his navel. He stands on the altar and stretches as in a dream ballet. The music bursts forth, and the graffitti-bearers, immobile before, rush forward, seize the altar-figure and hold him aloft, circle the altar, lay him upon it and pile in on him in a frenzy of writhing limbs.

Then, with one deafening note from a bass drum, the music stops. Stillness. The graffitti-bearers return to their places, replace their clothing, and are seated again in prayerful attitudes. A woman or child in the congregation stands and says without emotion, 'He was wounded for our transgressions, he was bruised for our iniquities; the Lord has laid on him the sin of us all'. The minister in the front stands and says, 'Go home'.[2]

Go home! I should have thought the door stewards would be pounded to jelly in the rush. Dr Killinger does comment that this is a radical departure from customary forms of worship and that he would be nervous if asked to take part in such a service. Which makes two of us!

In honesty, I admit to being irredeemably conservative in matters of liturgy. Worse still, I used to be downright slipshod in preparing a service, spending hours finding the exact pattern of words to address at the congregation through the sermon whilst casually throwing together a few sentences to be directed to God in worship. This is the Nonconformist malaise, and I had a bad case of it. The liturgy was little more than a frame around the sermon which formed the picture—though any art expert could have pointed out that an ill-chosen frame would transform a masterpiece into a nondescript daub.

I had a bad start. My earliest memories were of mahogany pews with squeaking doors, an aspidistra in a hideous urn

[2] J. Killinger, *Leave It to the Spirit* (Harper & Row, 1971)

on the communion table and WORSHIP THE LORD IN THE BEAUTY OF HOLINESS in flaking paint above the pulpit. Only much later did I learn that *liturgy* means 'the work of the people'. We didn't do any; just sat like blocks of wood except when we rose to sing hymns or recited the Lord's Prayer. For the rest, the preacher got on with it, telling God in prayers of interminable length what was happening in His own world and telling us in the sermon what miserable sinners we were and how Drink was ruining the nation. An hilarious time was had by all. Had it not been for a nubile soprano with a saucy eye in the choir I should probably have been a happy atheist by now. Things changed when we were placed in the care of a daring young minister who wore a gown, smoked in the minister's vestry and (horror of horrors!) addressed the Almighty as 'You'. He also crossed himself when pronouncing the Blessing—and any Primitive Methodist can tell you what *that's* a symptom of! My count against him was different. When eventually he took himself off to the Anglicans, he carried with him the undying affection of the choir soprano. Now, no doubt, she is judging the marmalade competition at the parish fete and presiding graciously at the rector's table when he entertains the bishop. . . .

. . . However, enough of this maudlin reminiscence, otherwise I shall break down and sob. Liturgism is the debasement of liturgy because it depends more upon the antics of the preacher than the work of the people. It is not worship but theatre, and although there is a place for that in church (after all, that's where it originated) one must really draw the line at burlesque. Gimmickry may add to the congregation, especially in those communities described by Dylan Thomas as 'Bible-black and cavern-cold' where the cinemas are shut on Sundays, but will subtract from the fullness of true worship.

The liturgical Word is both the word which the ordered

Christian community addresses to its Lord, and his Word to the world mediated through the Church. It is the form of the Church preaching, the stance of the Church listening, the posture of the Church doing homage. The sermon demands a trumpet; liturgy requires a full orchestra, and as we noted in Dr Killinger's somewhat bizarre example described above, the whole range of human senses may be employed—sight, sound, taste, smell and touch. It is the antithesis of the extreme proclamation-situation where a preacher seeks to project neat rows of passive souls in the direction of the Kingdom of Heaven on wings of rhetoric. Movement, music, silence, visual images and tangible objects may all have an honourable place in the Work of the People. But there must be some context of discipline for, in liturgy as in life, Paul's advice is, as a general rule, sound, 'Let your moderation be known to all men'. There will always be exceptions when the People of God respond to some act of God's Grace with spontaneous hallelujahs. But such ejaculations must be extemporaneous: they cannot be contrived.

We are passing, many of us with shattered ear-drums and outraged dignity, through an era of liturgical experimentation. The solutions of the *avant garde* may sometimes be spurious but the problem to which they are addressing themselves is a real one. The great, classical liturgies of the Church are phrased in language as mellifluous as it is meaningless to twentieth-century man. Certainly there is comfort in the strictest sense to be derived from entering into the experience of the saints of every age, and we affirm the essential integrity of the Church when we rehearse the sayings of Jesus and those who have followed him through Christian history. It is worth sacrificing a modicum of meaning to identify oneself with so rich a tradition.

Yet it is precisely history that the liturgical experimenters would claim to have on their side. The worship of the earliest Christians had no fixed form. Formal liturgies, other than those carried over from the Jewish tradition, only came into being after the lapse of time. In the worship of Jesus as Lord anything went—within limits. Corinth was admittedly an extreme case, but there is abundant evidence that variety, spontaneity and freedom were the marks of the worship of the Apostolic Church. It had only one fixed formula—the Lord's Prayer, and even then there were two versions depending upon whether you took Matthew or Luke as your authority. Worship was Spirit-inspired, and the Holy Spirit impels those who open themselves to him to do the oddest things. Gratitude and joy were the twin key-signatures of Apostolic worship with expectant hope underlying both; the hope articulated by Paul in his letter to the Romans, 'He who did not spare his own Son but gave him up for us all, will he not also give us all things with him?'

In the words of a leading New Testament scholar, Floyd Filson, 'The Church's worship had no rigid pattern. Great variety was the constant fact. Freedom was axiomatic.' So the more stiff-necked theologians who are prepared to go to the stake to support their theories about the exact liturgical slot the Prayer of Thanksgiving should occupy may be able to invoke the authority of Chrysostom, Justin Martyr or Clement of Alexandria, but they have the Holy Spirit to reckon with. Worship is prior to theology in the New Testament. The Church was first and foremost a worshipping fellowship of believers, and its formal thinking expresses the convictions and world-view implicit in its faith and worship. Clear thinking may correct faulty worship, but in the Christian life worship precedes explicit theology.

Furthermore, liturgy is the rhythm of real life, and this fact can create problems for both traditionalists and innovators. Because no one in his right mind speaks in the cadences and vocabulary of Elizabethan English except as a recitation of a formal liturgy, worship can easily part company with the everyday world and become something the believer does in a hallowed setting, at a special time and using phrases associated with an esoteric ritual. It was Dietrich Bonhoeffer who condemned the German Churches of the 1930s for avoiding a confrontation with the evils of Nazism by retreating into liturgism. He put the issue in one sentence— 'Only he who cries out for the Jews dare permit himself to sing in Gregorian!' The Liturgical Word is first and foremost God speaking through a Prophetic Fellowship to the world before it is the Christian Community addressing God in the language of worship on behalf of the world.

And if the definition of liturgy as the rhythm of real life be permitted, it makes nonsense of much that passes for worship in contemporary idiom. Is it truly an expression of the rhythm of real life for the average churchgoer to dance down the aisle with a daffodil behind his ear singing 'Lord of the Dance'? To be sure, anything which gets on the move those pews-full of wooden soldiers has something to commend it. But they have to be shown cause for genuine celebration in their daily lives before they can 'dance before the Lord'. And this must mean exposure to the Gospel in all its freshness and power—liberation and renewal at the pressure-points of life, sex, money, power, ambition, politics, justice—in a word, *conversion*. Which brings us back inevitably to that old-fashioned functionary, the preacher. There are those who can claim to have been born again by the Holy Spirit acting through dance, dialogue and drama. But someone has to pose the question and demand a response. 'How shall they hear without a preacher?' Indeed, *what* will they hear other than cacophony if some of our more extreme liturgical experimenters have their way?

My claim would be that the Liturgical Word is not pious, magical or secretive in meaning. It is evangelical, prophetic and public. Whether the words be those of Cranmer or Michel Quoist, the music that of Bach or Andrew Lloyd Webber, the aim must be the transfiguration of ordinary life by the Kingdom of God. And the acid test of relevance is that proposed by Paul to the Church at Corinth: 'If the whole congregation is assembled and some uninstructed persons or unbelievers should enter, will they think you are mad? But if the visitor when he enters, hears from everyone something that searches his conscience and brings conviction, the secrets of his heart are laid bare. So he will fall down and worship God crying, "God is certainly among you!"' The nub of the issue is not to turn verbal or ritual somersaults in order to attract the outsider, but to speak a Liturgical Word which *if* an outsider should stray into Christian worship, he will observe the Gospel in action and be aware that the kingdoms of this world are being transformed into the Kingdom of God and of his Son, Jesus Christ. He ought to find it hard to remain a spectator.

Whilst I admire the courage and imaginativeness of those parsons or groups of laity who put tremendous effort and dedication into the task of livening up moribund church Services in an honourable attempt to attract outsiders, I am afraid their liturgical innovations often go just far enough to irritate the faithful but not far enough to ensnare the godless. Stating it crudely, setting 'The Old Rugged Cross' to a Beatle's tune is not a genuine liturgical innovation. For the key question is not: is the tune an expression of modern culture, but, what do the words mean? And how can we identify ourselves with Christ's sacrifice in the life of the world?

By the same token I have reservations about volumes of 'with-it' prayers such as those of Malcolm Boyd or Michel Quoist. I freely admit my reaction is strictly subjective because I know many people have been helped by them. Yet when I hear one of these stark, scathing prayers used in

public worship, I can't help calling to mind Phillips Brooks'
pointed comment about one of his fellow-preachers who
'uttered one of the finest prayers ever offered to a Boston
audience'. Undoubtedly Boyd and Quoist spare their hearers
nothing of the sordid reality of life outside the protective
walls of the dignified sanctuary. To bring the pain, disease
and misery of the world to the attention of those churchgoers who wish to escape from it to be apart with God can
be no bad thing. But there is a fundamental difference
between reluctant guilt and true contrition: hang-dog shame
is a trivial attitude for Man the sinner confronted by the
holiness of God. Prayer should surely be addressed to God,
through the congregation possibly, but ought not to rebound
in his direction *off* the congregation, propelled by strong
words or even stronger emotions. I suppose I am being less
than fair to Malcolm Boyd and Michel Quoist, and if we are
at odds it is because I regard as sermons what they would
classify as prayers. Yet does the distinction matter so long
as they succeed in bringing liturgy to life?

What does matter is that too many contemporary liturgies
fail to achieve their purpose because the language employed
is too trivial to bear the weight of mystery. This is not to
imply that mystery is synonymous with unintelligibility;
that the Liturgical Word ought to be couched in the majestic
if convoluted English of the Authorised Version if it is to
qualify for religious use. A congregation should understand
clearly what it is saying or what is being said on its behalf
otherwise it is engaged in magic rather than worship. But
clarity is not the same thing as superficiality. The translators
of modern versions of the Bible have shown that it is possible
to express God's Word in the language of the people without robbing it of dignity. Granted, translating the Bible is
a task for experts, whereas many modern liturgies are the
product of working parsons or small groups of Christians
whose basic skills may not include mastery of the spoken or

written word. So be it. They are not required to change what is said so much as bring out the meaning of what is done—for that is 'liturgy'—the work of the people. To do this, they need not be liturgiologists, able to quote passages of Dom Gregory Dix's monumental *The Shape of the Liturgy* in their sleep. If they have the Gospel they can find the words so long as they struggle for strong, clear, simple English and do not settle for slovenliness.

In the last resort liturgy is concerned not with words or emotions but with truth. The unspoken question which presses in upon every Christian when he shares in the ritual of the gathered community is quite simply—is God worth worshipping? Or put differently, what kind of God do we really believe in? For worship cannot be faked. In the words of John Austin Baker:

> The vacancy of mind, the lack of attention, the concern with petty trivialities, the surges of superstitious awe or emotional enthusiasm ungeared to the business of living, the critical appraisal of other worshippers and of those 'taking the service', which characterize so many churchgoers at their devotions are not to be ascribed primarily to human weakness. They correspond with terrifying honesty to the vagueness and remoteness of the concept of God, to a failure to face the profound moral challenge on which belief must rest, to an immense indifference to the implications of belief.[3]

Strong words, but undoubtedly true. We reveal the dimensions of the God in which we believe by our attitude to worship; and more, we betray the quality of our discipleship and our passion or lack of it for God's Kingdom. Contrast that all-too familiar situation described by John Baker with the profound theological understanding of probably the greatest Free Church thinker of the past century, P. T. Forsyth. Commenting on the Eucharist, he said, 'When you

[3] J. A. Baker, *The Foolishness of God* (John Knox Press, 1975)

reflect after Communion, "What have I done today?" say to yourself, "I have done more than on any busiest day of the week. I have yielded myself to take part with the Church in Christ's finished Act of Redemption, which is greater than the making of the world." ' Let the worship be ordered or free, the language ornate or simple, the hymns ancient or modern, the setting tuppenny coloured or penny plain, it is a conception of God in his world as magnificent as that described by P. T. Forsyth which the Liturgical Word must embody. Capture that vision, harness that power, and worship will burst out of the walls of the sanctuary and the work of the people of God, known technically as *liturgy*, will be dedicated to transforming the life of our society, which is the sphere of our reasonable service.

We are in urgent need of a liturgical revival (which is not necessarily the same as liturgical revolution) not for its own sake, nor for the Church's sake, but for the sake of a world poverty-stricken in spirituality and starved of saving truth. The Liturgical Word is a paean of praise, a volume of intercession which encompasses all God's children, and above all, an act of dedication to the cause of God's Kingdom.

2 *The Sacramental Word*

There is one thing in common between the Liturgical and Sacramental Words other than their historical and theological relationship—both are independent of the oratorical or homiletical gifts of the individual preacher. They are the complete answer to pulpit subjectivism. Whatever damage an incompetent or, worse, popular but glib preacher may do, it can be repaired by the People of God themselves through the agency of these rites. Where he is churchy, they are worldly; when he harps on his pet theme with monotonous regularity, they deploy the whole range of Christian truth; if he submerges his congregation beneath a torrent of words, they will dry it out through a number of simple actions. Above all, should his God-given authority degenerate into insufferable arrogance, liturgy and sacrament will cut him down to size and elevate Christ. There is nothing he can do which sacraments cannot do better, except possibly explain themselves. *That* modest task *is* reserved to the preacher— to educate his people into a true understanding of the central importance of the Liturgical and Sacramental Word. And if he is an honest man, not smitten with the blight of clericalism, he will point out that liturgy is normative of ministry. This is where the doctrine of the Priesthood of All Believers has the dust blown off it and is given practical effect.

My intention is not to set the preacher's role in contrast with or even contradiction to the function of the Liturgical and Sacramental Words. For these ordinances of God do not merely correct his faults and expose his temptations but also strengthen his ministry and fortify his spiritual life. He can so easily preach himself empty; become so impatient with his people that he finds it difficult to look them in the face from the pulpit, or more likely, be so busy doing his job for Christ's sake that he loses touch with them. The preacher is in frequent need of a reminder that he is not Atlas carrying the world on his back; that God's scheme of Salvation is not totally dependent upon him. At such times, the preacher must be able to descend from his lofty eyrie, that loneliest of places on earth, the pulpit, and join his people, listening rather than speaking, taking instead of giving, being carried with them rather than driving them towards that darkness which is Light. There is more than physical relief to be gained from a change in stance— shoulder to shoulder rather than face to face contact with his congregation. His special interest may be liturgical renewal but his deepest need is for regular personal regeneration. God offers it through the Sacramental Word.

The Word and The Words

(i) Holy Communion

I address myself as a preacher to preachers. I have neither the courage nor competence to prod the writhing snakes' nest of theological and historical controversies associated with the sacrament of the Lord's Supper. Suffice it to say that I do not come to the Lord's Table trusting either in my own righteousness or someone else's wisdom. I am in awe of those great theologians who claim to know what happens, if anything, to the bread and wine when the Words of Consecration are said over them. They are not only cleverer men than I am but also braver. I would as soon play with forked lightning as be dogmatic about *that* matter, which seems to me to rest firmly within the area of God's sovereign prerogative. I am as agnostic about the composition of the sacramental elements as I would be nervous at tackling the exotic and unfamiliar cuisine served up at a friend's table. But provided I trusted the host, I would eat gratefully. And for me, the Host is not the material held aloft by some priest at a given point in the Eucharist. The Host is the one who invites me to the feast and presides at the table—the living Christ, present through his Spirit which binds together the company of his followers in a *sacramentum*—an oath of allegiance to follow him to Hell and back and share in his self-giving for all mankind.

And whilst I am clearing out things I do *not* believe about Holy Communion, I am sure that many Christians besides myself are 'turned off' by the imagery of the traditional Office. I find the injunction to 'eat Christ's flesh and drink his blood' frankly repellent, even as a metaphor. Similarly, terms such as *satisfaction*, *propitiation* and *oblation* latch on to nothing in the experience and thought-world of modern man. The liturgical reformers who have retired Cranmer to a place of honour in the ecclesiastical museum have done the Church a signal service. His Prayer of Consecration, for

100

example, though grammatically correct, as one would expect
from an Archbishop who had a sadistic schoolmaster, is so
bedevilled by subordinate clauses as to be virtually unread-
able in public. It also concentrates massively upon the
atoning death of Jesus to the exclusion of his Resurrection.
We share the Last Supper of the old Creation but are denied
a seat at the first Breakfast of the New Age.

These quibbles apart, faulty teaching or no teaching at all
ensures that Holy Communion remains a minority obser-
vance in Nonconformity. There is the erroneous impression,
reinforced by the barbaric habit of tacking a mutilated
version of it on to the end of the main Service, that it is a
form of spiritual freemasonry. Sinners slink quietly away
whilst the saints stay behind to undergo the Rite of the
Righteous. Most parsons, trying to persuade some fringer
or other to remain for Communion, have been told that the
defector is 'not good enough'. And it is a tough job to
convince such a person of humble pretensions that his
reason is precisely the wrong one; that Holy Communion is
'for sinners only'. But the misconception dies hard.

There is also a strong conviction on the part of some
Christian activists that Holy Communion is an especially
spiritual rite, designed for those who seek to get away from
the world and be with God. The idea that the communion
table is not the assembly point for a mystical retreat but the
place where the manifold activity of the world is symbolized
in the bread and wine upon it does not commend itself to
many traditional Christians. With disastrous results, they
project a view of holiness which is neither scriptural nor
contemporary. They genuinely desire to escape from the
world for a while to be with God and so, however unwit-
tingly, drive away those who can find God only at the centre
of life.

What, then, are the marks of the truly Sacramental Word?
I and thousands of others owe a great debt to Bishop John

Robinson who has that rare ability to bring Biblical theology within the range of the common man and cast fresh light on perennial truths. I have steeped myself in his writings and would advise apprentice-preachers to do the same. In some parts of the analysis which follows I lean heavily on his *Liturgy Coming to Life* (S.C.M. 1960).

The Liturgical Word, as we have seen, concerns something done by the people rather than anything said by the preacher. It is the Gospel in action. The Eucharist is neither said nor sung; it is *done*. And the thing which is done first and foremost is God's saving act in Christ to renew the world—a work once finished but whose power is made operative in every time and place through the Church. The Eucharist points both backwards and forwards—to what Christ has done for the world at Golgotha and to what he wills to do in the 'last hour' between Resurrection and Consummation. It is also done in the perpetual present as those who believe in him are invited to enter into his death and resurrection. The form it takes is a re-enactment of the Last Supper, the common meal where the historical Jesus shared with the disciples his looming fate and challenged them to share it. The actual liturgical shape matters little so long as the people understand what is being done and why. The Scriptural Words of Institution are used to anchor firmly what is happening to its roots in the Incarnation and also ensure the continuity throughout the centuries which guarantees the Church's integrity. But we must beware lest our habitual use of the term 'memorial' gives undue weight to the past. It is the future which is the most important dimension for the Christian. He looks for the coming of the Kingdom and the time when sacraments will be rendered nugatory by the transformation of history into a new Creation which will be wholly sacramental; 'alive with his life' as Paul puts it.

Hence, the Eucharist as the Protestant understands it can

never be a priestly office. According to the usage of the early Church, the celebrant was neither Bishop nor presbyter but the 'president'—one of the people chosen to ensure that things were done in due order. The people themselves celebrated; the president added nothing by way of magical power to what was done. To sharpen the distinction between president and priest—the president is the sergeant-major seeing the troops are drawn up for battle; the priest is a gladiator, doing combat in the arena with the people watching the spectacle. When we talk of 'building' the Kingdom of God (a verb, incidentally, of liberal vintage and foreign to the New Testament) the standard model is not that of Christians engaged in every aspect of the life of society, though this is an essential dimension of their discipleship, but the Eucharist which, as John Robinson points out, is *the* distinctive Christian social action. All else flows from it.

According to this view of the Eucharist, the communicants are co-celebrants not with the priest or minister but with Christ. Jesus' command is explicit and to the point—'This do ye. . . .' And what they do is spelled out in four, simple, active verbs. They *take* bread and wine, tokens of God's creation and man's work upon it. The bread symbolizes the whole economic life of the world, the innumerable processes from planting through manufacturing to selling, the labour of men's hands and brains, embracing industry, commerce, trade unionism and consumption. The wine is a token of all that is not strictly functional in the world—joy, leisure, laughter, friendship, conviviality. The elements are a microcosm of God's Creation, over which Man has been given dominion, and they are handed back to Christ for his purposes, to become the raw material of his Kingdom. How, then, can we possibly claim that in Holy Communion we get away from the world for a while to be with God? The world is right there on the communion

103

table, which is less an altar than a workman's bench. Nor can we allow that the Lord's Supper falls within the context of the doctrine of Redemption. The Christian doctrine of Creation is central to the rite. That is where it begins.

The second active verb is *bless*. It is a fallen world, a warped Creation within which we live, and that must be regenerated. Bread does not only symbolize honest toil but also graft and greed; the exploitation of millions for the satisfaction of a minority. We cannot hold that piece of bread in our hands without recalling those who have no bread; whose life is one of grinding poverty and malnutrition. And the wine is not only the fruit of joy but the poison of excess, the cause of degradation, the misuse of leisure, the betrayal of friendship—in sum: moral degeneration. These simple elements, so apparently benign, are parables of the harsh truth that something has gone badly wrong with the world; that the whole created Order is in dire need of redemption. Christ cannot use what we give him without transforming it, restoring it to its original pristine splendour through his blessing. The bread and wine, the teeming life of the world, has to be reclaimed by God through identification with the saving work of Christ. Hence; his declaration —'This flawed material, this soured wine is my body and blood.' The Old Testament imagery appropriated by the New Testament is unmistakable, 'Behold the Lamb of God that taketh away the sin of the world!'

If *blessing* is what has to be done, then *breaking* is how it must be done. The broken body of Christ and his spilled blood draws us to the foot of the Cross to observe an act of self-sacrifice. One may challenge the statement in Hebrews that 'without the spilling of blood there can be no forgiveness' and quote Scripture against itself by reciting the parables of the Prodigal Son or the Lost Sheep where forgiveness was offered without a trip to the charnel house. But in the realm where deeds of cosmic significance are done, the rules are transcended. The breaking of the bread which has become part of Christ is the kernel of the Christian doctrine of Redemption. It says more and says it more vividly, that simple act, than all the theories of the Atonement. We are witnesses to the incalculable power of the self-sacrifice of Cosmic Man, the Omega-point of human evolution—to use the language of Teilhard de Chardin. Christ was obedient unto death. The next move is God's, and those who shared that Last Supper could not comprehend what it might be, in spite of Jesus' prophetic words, until Easter Day.

The fourth verb transforms spectators into participants. It is the *sharing* of the bread and wine that Christ has taken, blessed and broken. 'Every one of you eat this; drink this'— if you dare! We undergo the harrowing and suffering of entering into Christ's sacrifice as individuals, but it is as a fellowship, a Church, we rise to fresh life. The nucleus of a new people of God has been formed from those who, in however pedestrian a fashion, have expressed their willingness to share his sacrifice by eating the bread and drinking the wine. What we could never do and be as individuals we can accomplish as those who have together identified themselves with the death of Christ and by so doing have died to self in order to rise to live for others. The simple act of sharing the loaf and cup is a covenant bond stronger than any legalistic contract the world could devise. As Paul puts it, 'Because there is one loaf, we who are many are one body.' In the words of John Robinson: 'The Last Supper was the dress rehearsal for the first supper of the new age, when the risen Lord would with them eat the bread and drink the cup new in his kingdom, and life would begin afresh in the resurrection order brought into being by Good Friday, Easter and Whitsun.'

Of course every attempt to use the crude medium of words to penetrate the heart of the Eucharist only serves to increase the mystery even if it does not increase the puzzlement of the average Christian, who finds himself floundering without a lifebelt in the great theological deeps. But this is surely the beauty of the Eucharist. What exhausts language and in the end defies explanation, can be contained in a series of simple actions held together by one simple phrase— 'Do *this*!' Do it, and leave the rest to God.

So in the Eucharist we have the power of great preaching which needs no great preacher. Just a group of people who take upon themselves the awesome responsibility for the whole world.

(ii) Baptism

To state the obvious: the theme of this book is preaching. And it is necessary to state the obvious so as to be able, with some degree of integrity, to side-step many of the perennial arguments about baptism. It is not the concern of the preacher *qua* preacher to adjudicate between infant and believers' baptism—presumably he made his mind up about that one when he took out a membership ticket of one Church rather than another. Nor need he be qualified to offer authoritative opinions about the genuineness of the Trinitarian formula in Matthew 28:19, or whether Jesus himself initiated the rite. Those are headaches for the Biblical scholars, and they are welcome to them. The preacher has enough of his own. And on the vexed question whether all children, including those of non-Christian parents, should be baptized—whatever decision he defends from the pulpit as a preacher he will already have settled elsewhere as a pastor.

The preacher need only satisfy himself on a few principles before joining with his people in proclaiming the Baptismal Word. The sacrament of baptism in whatever form marks the entry of the individual into the Church of Christ. All Churches are agreed about that, with the exception of the

Society of Friends and the Salvation Army—and one must reluctantly dissent from their convictions in a spirit of of Christian charity. Secondly, Christ may or may not have instituted the rite, but he has certainly continued it through his Church in an unbroken tradition down to the present day. Thirdly, God, so the Bible asserts, has a plan for mankind. Is he likely to exclude children from it? The central tradition of reformed Christianity has always claimed that the Church consists of all professing believers and their children. Does not the shadow of the Cross also cover 'his little ones'—whether infants in faith or age? Are they to be denied that new life which floods into the world through the Resurrection until they reach some arbitrary determined age? What a joyless place will the Kingdom of God be if there are no children in it! None of these assertions is to deny the validity of believers' baptism; merely to challenge its claim to exclusiveness.

Much of the controversy surrounding baptism arises from misguidedly asking the wrong question, which is: what good can a child receive from a rite whose meaning he is too young to comprehend? Put that way, the answer is 'None!' Baptism has neither the prophylactic value of vaccination—one jab and you are safe for life—nor the cultic significance of a magical ceremony. It is not a new gift of Christ to the child but the re-affirmation of Christ's perpetual gift to his Church of which the child has become a member. Baptism is a proclamation to the Church and through the Church to the world that all men live, move and have their being in God. And this is not a privilege they acquire through baptism; the Church baptizes them because they have it. Certainly many may, like the child in later life, repudiate the claim, but they cannot deny the fact. It is writ in the heavens and recorded in earthly history; it *is* earthly history—the story of mankind seen from the perspective of God.

Those who charge that infant baptism is meaningless because the child cannot, in any theological sense have faith, are not only attacking what is not being defended but they are denying the priority of grace over faith. And that is bad theology, at least in the view of those who are heirs of the Reformation. Faith is the gift of God's grace. And there is no prescribed interval between the gift—grace, and the response—faith. Infant baptism is not rendered invalid if there is no individual faith in the recipient. It most certainly would be if both Church and child were in any sense outside the realm of God's grace. But if that were the case, not only would baptism be pointless but the whole Gospel, for Church, worship, sacraments, preaching and the totality of Christian discipleship are predicated upon the ever-present power of God's regenerating grace.

The Word and the Sacraments are the two great expressions of the Gospel in worship; the one, the Gospel audible; the others, the Gospel visible. And just as the Gospel does not become untrue if a man rejects it, so Baptism is not invalid should a child be unable to understand it. In either case the act is God's, his self-bestowal to the Church and through the Church to all mankind. So baptism is the authoritative symbol of an eternal fact; a truth of eternity penetrating time. That fact was true before baptism, and without baptism—every human being by virtue of being born into a redeemed world is a potential member of the Christian Church. Baptism proclaims children sons or daughters of God; it does not make them so. Christ did that. The Gospel announces redemption for all men. Baptism applies it.

Such a concept of baptism cannot live with any individualistic theology. It is not primarily an act of the parents, or of the child, but of the Church, and of Christ in the Church. Certainly there is value in the stamp of God's property being marked on the child in the sign of the Cross, with the declaration that he is offered publicly to God, having been born to be born again, pronounced by right a citizen of the Kingdom of God. Naturally, there is great solemnity in the promises made by parents, god-parents and the assembled congregation that they will together do everything within their power to see that he does not forfeit his birthright. But we still lose something of the real significance of baptism if we show more interest in the recipient than in the Church that administers it. The sacrament of baptism is something which *happens* to the child, but it is *done* by the Church. To enter into one's inheritance at baptism is not to receive an individual tincture of grace from the hands of a priest acting instead of the Church, but to have it affirmed that one has a share in the common destiny of the Church at the hands of a minister acting on behalf of the Church, and in its presence.

What, then, is the nub of the matter when we talk of the baptismal Word as preaching? It is, in the words of P. T. Forsyth, the recognition that every infant baptism is sympathetically an adult baptism. The baptism of every infant ought to be a reaffirmation of the baptism of every adult present. The entire congregation go back to the meaning of their own baptism, examining themselves to see how far they have kept the faith for which they were once claimed and clung to the Cross by which they were bought. Has the innocence of infancy grown into the moral purity of Christian maturity? Has the water become spirit and the kindling caught fire? The whole Church revives by faith its sense of eternal forgiveness and professes by the same faith its place in the New Creation.

Writes Forsyth: 'In a practical sense the whole Church of the baptized undergo adult baptism at each infant baptism. They do consciously what they were put through unconsciously at the first. They are not *spectators* of a baptism—they *assist*. And they do not only assist, they *participate* in the baptism. They *take up* their own baptism, as you might take up actually a citizenship, or a freedom, long yours by right.'[4]

Luther, whenever he was depressed or under strong attack and sensed his courage failing, would say to himself, '*Baptizatus sum*'—'I was baptized'. Thus he gained encouragement not only from the awareness that the complete baptismal event extended throughout his life, but felt himself, though physically isolated, part of the company of the universal Church. Here was the great Reformer, not thundering at his congregation from the pulpit in Wittenberg, but receiving the comfort and challenge of the Church through the Sacramental Word—the preacher having the Gospel preached to him.

The strength of Sacramental Words as preaching is that they do not depend upon the eloquence of a preacher or the orthodoxy of his theology. They are not subject to his whims and moods. Nor is the size of the congregation of much importance, even less its frame of mind, bored or rebellious, restless or sycophantic. The *prima donna* of the pulpit need not pull out all the stops of his virtuosity because his reputation has preceded him. Alternatively, should he be so fuzzy of thought or slip-shod in verbal expression that he only succeeds in projecting his own doubts and confusions upon his hearers, they need not stagger out of the church doors having endured the discipline, godly or otherwise, of aching brains and sore backs instead of the exhilaration of warmed hearts. At such times, Christ will have preached at communion table or font whilst we have been darkening counsel in the pulpit.

[4] P. T. Forsyth, *The Church and the Sacraments*, p. 182 (London, 1917)

SEVEN

The Word—Structured yet Spontaneous

I RECENTLY read somewhere—'The sermon is out; preaching is in' a neat half-truth which encapsulates the widely held opinion that highly stylized pulpit rhetoric of the type summarized by the Negro preacher, 'First I explains the text, then I presents the argyments, then I puts in the rousements', has had its day. Is the sermon as antiquated a vehicle for conveying the Gospel as Jesus' donkey, John Wesley's coach or Professor H. R. Mackintosh's Model T Ford in which he hurtled down Edinburgh's Princes Street, terrorizing pedestrians who lacked the great theologian's eschatological confidence? Even Professors of Preaching seem to think so: thus Dr John Killinger:

> People obviously believe in communication. What they don't believe in is some functionary paid to wear a black robe and stand behind a funny old desk and bore them with truisms, clichés and platitudes about beauty, life and truth while they twiddle their thumbs and squirm for the hour to be over so they can get to the golf course or the picnic grounds or the televized ball game. . . .[1]

That picture is tinged with parody. Many preachers, far from belching forth truisms, clichés and platitudes about beauty, truth and life, have sweated their guts out trying to

[1] J. Killinger, *Leave It to the Spirit* (Harper & Row, 1971)

find something worth saying and the best way of saying it. And if they *are* functionaries, then the parsons amongst them are economic masochists—they could earn more as street sweepers. And lay preachers are surely entitled to a relaxing Sunday after a hard week's work, without sacrificing their leisure-time to the hard graft of sermon construction and the even more taxing effort of putting it across. But grant Dr Killinger's main point. The sermonic form *is* out of fashion and too many sermons *are* a test of congregational endurance rather than a challenge to congregational intellect and conscience.

One cannot condone bad craftsmanship on the grounds that a high vocation excuses a low score. Yet the antithesis stated in the claim that though the sermon is 'out', preaching is 'in', can only be defended when pulpit style becomes a parody of itself in the manner beloved of music-hall comedians. Twenty-five years ago, Dr W. E. Sangster, in a standard work on preaching, allowed himself a *jeu d'esprit* by translating a well-known nursery rhyme into the argot of the most horrendous of pulpiteers:

> Mother Hubbard you see, was old; there being no mention of others, we may presume she was alone; a widow—a friendless, solitary widow. Yet did she despair? *Did* she despair? Did she sit down and weep, or read a novel or wring her hands? No! *She went to the cupboard.* Note that: she *went* to the cupboard. She did not hop, skip, jump or use any other peripatetic artifice; she solely and simply *went* to the cupboard. And why did she go to the cupboard? Was it to bring forth golden goblets, or glittering precious stones, or costly apparel, or any other attributes of wealth? No! *It was to get her dog a bone!* Not only was the widow poor, but her dog, the sole prop of her old age, was poor too. . . .[2]

In sharper vein, the mock sermon on the text, 'For Esau was a hairy man but I am a smooth man' from the satirical

[2] W. E. Sangster, *The Craft of Sermon Construction* (Baker Books, 1972)

review *Beyond the Fringe* was near enough to the knuckle to
set up echoes in the minds of most preachers who now blush
at the memory of their early attempts to master the art of
the sermon. Yet the fact that a form of communication so
readily lends itself to lampoon does not invalidate it, though
it certainly forces the preacher to *listen* to himself as he talks,
sensitive to cadence of speech, sogginess of structure and
sheer quality of content.

The sermon may not be the only way of proclaiming the
Word of God, but it antedates all others so it cannot lightly
be dismissed as having outlived its usefulness without closer
examination. It is obviously a structure that has acquired
layers of barnacles over time which must be stripped off
before its essential form can be revealed. It is, I suspect,
these accretions which make radical critics write off the
sermon as old-fashioned or even grotesque, and often with
good cause. But the essence of preaching is quite another
matter. If the work of sermon-making is honestly done, then
what is said approximates as closely as the human spirit and
intellect can get to some central theme of God's Word. And
that cannot be written off, however much critics object or
ordinary folk fail to hear.

1 *The Structured Word*

Having affirmed the historical precedence of the sermon as
the vehicle of God's Word, I do not claim a monopoly for
it. Drama, dance, dialogue, music and even silence have all
occupied the slot traditionally reserved for the sermon in
modern liturgies. And it would be utterly presumptuous of
me to suggest that any or all of these alternatives are mere
fads or 'way-out' attempts to achieve by gimmickry what
the sermon has apparently failed to do—capture the imagination and engage the attention of our generation. The Trad
too easily damns the Trendy for filling old ruts with new

rubbish. Yet who dare put limits on the sovereign freedom of God's Spirit to use anyone or anything in the whole Created Order to accomplish the Divine purpose? As Paul recognized, Christians are debtors both to Greeks and Barbarians and it is not orthodoxy but arrogance to deny it.

However, though I doff my cap to those brave spirits who are seeking to set out God's Word by experimenting with materials and means of communication which traditional churchgoers find shocking or profane, I confess I lack the courage or competence to do the same. I struggle at the business of being a preacher, trying to expound the Word of God through the medium of formal speech—the sermon, in fact. I freely acknowledge it is not the only way, but it is my way, and this cobbler intends to stick to his last. Christian publicists who wish to learn more about contemporary alternatives to the sermon are reading the wrong book. I have never, for example, engaged in dialogue within the context of Christian worship, whereas I have preached enough bad sermons to qualify for life-membership in the League of Militant Atheists. I have also heard enough sermons, good, bad and indifferent from other preachers to risk drawing some conclusions about this unique, and to the outsider, very odd form of communication.

True sermons are a paradoxical mixture of highly structured and yet spontaneous speech. Let's examine the structure now and deal with the spontaneity later.

Herewith an observation so profound that it leaves me gasping at my own originality. The preacher who has nothing to say will always achieve his objective. Eloquently, colourfully or (perish the thought!) boringly, he will say precisely nothing. If he is so inclined he will ransack the treasure-trove of English literature, enlisting to his aid every word artist from Shakespeare to T. S. Eliot. Intoxicated by the adrenalin pulsing through his system he may call down lightning from heaven or shake the pillars of the temple until the very earth quakes. With imagery so graphic that he has his congregation one moment vainly trying to contain their laughter and the next hold back their tears, he will press on to his chosen goal, and he will only choose *that* when he reaches his final sentence. Cut to the quick by his verbal thrusts and soothed by his winsome words, the congregation are, by turns, astonished at his scholarship and stunned by the range of his knowledge—science, the arts, current affairs, even a little theology. They will be spared nothing, for that is what he has to offer them and they are bound to get it. Like pseudo-art critics gazing in awe at a blank canvas in a gilded frame, the sermon-tasters will hail the advent of an extraordinary new talent. The rest are likely to scratch their heads and berate themselves at their stupidity in failing to realize that Paul's Epistle to the Hebrews was written by Apollos. All in all, the experience can only be compared to walking under a waterfall without getting wet.

I know whereof I speak. Too frequently I have climbed the pulpit steps with only the glimmer of an idea about the sermon I am about to inflict upon the congregation. On such occasions I am at my most eloquent, camouflaging the vacuum in my head under an elaborate web of words. And my relief when the Service is over is only exceeded by my bemusement at the number of congregational members who shake me warmly by the hand and thank me for my wonderful sermon!

In mitigation, I would submit it is a strangely mechanistic doctrine of the Holy Spirit to which the Church clings by its insistence that a Word from God, fully formed, will take up residence in the preacher's mind at 11 a.m. and 6.30 p.m. every Sunday, month in and month out. On reflection, there are times when I think the honest thing should have been to confess that God hadn't blessed me with any particular revelation that week and so there would be no sermon.

115

Quaker silence is infinitely more spiritually beneficial than the standard stratagem for occasions when the Divine messenger service has gone on strike—putting some lift in the left-overs, as the cookery manual has it, and rejuvenating an old homily.

I am being perverse since like a passably competent chess player I know the correct defence to that cheeky attack. But there are preachers who solemnly affirm the virtue of entering the pulpit with a totally blank mind and in their pre-sermon prayer inviting the Holy Spirit to fill it. Like the Devil they quote Scripture to support their case, usually the injunction of Jesus to his disciples, 'Take no thought how or what you shall speak; for it shall be given you in that same hour'. It is fundamentalism run riot to use that verse in defence of pulpit unpreparedness. Jesus was warning his followers about the inevitability of finding themselves dragged before the Government of the day and charged with sedition. In such a crisis, he advised, the best defence is not an academic discourse on the theology of the Civil Power, but personal testimony, memorably demonstrated centuries later by Martin Luther when he told the Diet of Worms, 'Here I stand. I can do no other!' That declaration has become immortal. It is unlikely that the average preacher will find himself in a comparable situation. Hence, he would be wise to base his approach to preaching on another command of Jesus—that we should love God with all our minds—which presumably involves study, thought and preparation.

Let us make the assumption that the preacher *has* something to say—a reasonable conjecture, otherwise he would be cleaning his car, fishing the nearest trout stream or lying in bed reading the Sunday newspapers. Then questions of sermon structure become important because effective communication is rarely a natural aptitude. It is generally achieved only by hard labour: that, plus a cool assessment of the combination of weaknesses and strengths which make us unique personalities rather than the endlessly uniform products of a single mould. It is impossible to divorce the preacher's character from what he says and how he says it. The sermon is *what* it is because the preacher is *who* he is. After all, the most famous of all definitions of preaching was given by Phillips Brooks in his Lyman-Beecher Lecture of 1876—'Preaching is the communication of truth by man to men through personality.'

Accept that definition and it is clear that every preacher either develops a style which is consonant with his personality, or else by default the quirks of his character will thrust a style upon him. Either *he* will preach the sermon or the sermon will preach *him*—which is all to the good if he can say with Paul, 'I live, yet not I, Christ lives in me'. Otherwise, he would be well advised to structure his sermons so as to neutralize his weaknesses and reinforce his strengths.

History has it that the Goths used to discuss their battle-plans, first, when they were drunk so they would not lack boldness, and again, the next morning, when they were sober so that hot-headed courage was tempered by cold-blooded prudence. Likewise, the preacher. His sermons need to be structured if the congregation are not to be at the mercy of his idiosyncracies but still feel that it is a flesh and blood human being who proclaims God's Word, and not a robot who hides a mass of transistorized circuitry beneath his Geneva gown.

My own observation for what it is worth is that too many sermons are indeed structured, but at the level of words rather than ideas. Having settled upon a theme, some preachers appear to jot down every mellifluous combination of sentences related to it their minds and memories can conjure up. One can visualize them, pen in hand, musing, 'That sounds good: put it down!' The result is a succession of purple passages linked together by pregnant pauses. It is the technique of the jerry-builder who lavishes his talent on the design of the wallpaper and hopes the steel girders that determine the shape and strength of the building will somehow or another link together by an act of God or *happenstance* as the Yanks call a lucky break which produces the same result as painstaking effort.

I indeed claimed earlier that the Word exists in the preacher's words, but not in *any* combination of words he cares to throw together because they tinkle tunefully upon the ear besides having some vague reference to the matter in hand. Too many preachers delight to splash around on the surface of things. Through mental laziness or moral timidity, we will not venture into the depths of a Biblical truth and then make the effort to tell what we have seen and learned in some kind of order so that our hearers can follow us step by step in reliving our experience. Jesus talked of cutting off hands and plucking out eyes—images of the raw agony of true spirituality. There is an anguish about authentic preaching—words are torn from the depths of a preacher's soul like the cries of a woman in childbirth rather than the gossipy ramblings of the village crone whose speech is a cascade of meritricious verbiage.

Milton talked of making his thoughts 'in harmonious numbers move'. More prosaically, I would echo this sentiment by arguing that the fundamental structure of the sermon is a progression of ideas which lead one after another to an irresistible conclusion. This is the end to which the sweat and blood of preaching is directed—hammering out a chain of linked concepts which may well occupy less than half a side of paper. But they *are* the sermon; all else is frippery; the pretty phrases, topical anecdotes, well-chosen quotations. When Jesus told his disciples to 'take no thought' he was certainly not advising them to do no thinking. Sheer brain-power is the essential pre-requisite of a well-wrought sermon, which is not to say that preaching demands an I.Q. of genius-level. The two-talent man can proclaim the Gospel with power, always provided that he invests both his talents in the preparation of it.

So leaving aside that mysterious, unpredictable element which God adds to preaching, a sermon is a skeleton of ideas fleshed out in words. And the aim is to 'body forth Christ', not to knock together some formless creature, all skin and bones; at worst a monster, at best a pathetic ghostly being likely to vanish in a puff of smoke at the first gust of the detractor's laughter.

Some public speakers over-estimate their hearers' powers of concentration; others do the opposite and insult the intelligence of a congregation. The only defence against either error is a strong, clear construct of ideas shaping the preached word so that long after the purple passages have faded from memory, the hearer can recapitulate the key theme and the development which flows from it.

This is probably the most appropriate point to dispose in a few sentences of an issue to which many works on preaching devote whole chapters. Shall the preacher use a verbatim manuscript, summary notes or speak extemporaneously? To be quite honest, I really do not regard the matter as materially significant. I have heard great preaching from men and women who have mastered each method. The important thing is not the impression the preacher conveys by his method of delivery, but what is left in the congregation's mind after he has finished. And it is to the skeletal structure of ideas that I would point, and insist that this is the imprint which should be burned like a brand into the brain of his hearers. Each method has its strengths, and its perils. A sermon delivered from a full manuscript can easily degenerate into a theological essay, paralytically dull unless the preacher brings to it something of his own personality, a directness which smashes through the paper barrier he would otherwise erect between himself and his hearers. An extemporaneous sermon, if there is such a creature, which I doubt, can have a congregation transfixed at the preacher's mastery of words, his acrobatic freedom in the pulpit, but when the performance is over, they sadly conclude, in James S. Stewart's pointed comment, that 'The Lord was not in the Wind'.

Every style has its dangers just as each preacher has his idiosyncracies. I would not dare to prescribe a standard method of address, any more than I have the right to pontificate about a preacher's style of dress. In each case the test is the same—attraction or distraction? For all I care, the preacher can wear a black and white dog-check suit, a Mickey Mouse tie and read from a faded parchment or appear in full canonicals and stride up and down the aisle to deliver himself of his oration. The only question that counts is: do the congregation hear the Word through his words? And a contingent question: will that Word live with them throughout the manifold cares and commitments of the following week? I offer only a one-word answer— *structure*. It is totally irrelevant whether unstructured speech issues from a full manuscript, partial notes or the tip of the preacher's tongue. Who can or cares to remember the outline of a shapeless mass of quivering verbal jelly? Yet who can forget a strong point driven home, sentence by sentence, until it pierces the listener to the heart?

There have been twentieth-century preachers, some of whose most famous sermons were obviously put together at the level of words rather than ideas. Peter Marshall is a good example. His method was essentially descriptive, the aim being to move his hearers by the emotive power of vivid narrative. He has sermons on both the Christmas and Easter themes which are essentially old stories brilliantly told. He argues no case but rather hopes to jolt his hearers into attention and from attention into allegiance by taking a Biblical incident which has lost its cutting edge through the attrition of constant usage and deck it out in fresh words that are the product of a rich imagination. There are respectable New Testament precedents for this method. But Peter Marshall was not only a born story-teller: he was a careful Scot, imbibing a sense of the integrity of Scripture with his mother's milk, so there was little danger of his mutilating the meaning of the original. The narrative preacher had better be quite sure that he is not doing badly what the Bible has already done well—dragging out at tedious length in colourless speech what Jesus, for example, captured in one gripping anecdote or a few crisp sentences. The ever-present peril is prolixity—the word-artist may take so long to set the scene, dress his sermon, as it were, with such painstaking care that it catches its death of cold. For those who are masters of words and are gifted with a disciplined imagination, the narrative sermon is a powerful option. Story tellers have conveyed truth in that way since the beginning of time. Lesser mortals would be well advised to use the technique sparingly.

To resume my main argument: a sermon structured at the level of ideas rather than words is only half the task; the other half is to take with the utmost seriousness a fact which is so glaringly obvious that it is often forgotten—ideas must be conveyed through the spoken rather than written word. Words were first invented to be voiced; only much later were they preserved on stone or parchment or paper. No one knows this better than the poet; thus, T. S. Eliot in 'Little Gidding':

> For last year's words belong to last year's language
> And next year's words await another voice.

But panting after the poet should come the preacher, always conscious that if he commits his sermon to paper, he is writing for the ear and not the eye. The majesty of Cranmer's English is only matched by the difficulty of speaking it. For example, the Prayer of Consecration in the Communion Service begins with a sentence 149 words long, boasting thirteen clauses, not counting the odd phrase in brackets. It is magnificent, but it is not spoken English. The celebrant needs not only the appropriate Godly gifts but also a mighty pair of lungs—and a compass would be useful as he battles his way from subject to object through a labyrinth of subordinate clauses.

Luther had the right idea. When he was translating the Bible, he collected popular ballads and songs, common tricks of speech used by the ordinary people—he put himself to school in the market place rather than the university. The result was the Word of God in the language of the masses. It is the Bible of the preacher rather than the pietist; at its best when trumpeted forth in public worship; less powerful when murmured in private devotion.

It is easy to exaggerate the difference between written and spoken words. *As a general rule*, he who murders grammar is granted no automatic pardon because he is speaking rather than writing English. But there are exceptions, a number of which are to be found in the Bible itself. The lay preacher who snorted when told the new minister was a Greek scholar and declared 'English was good enough for Paul; it's good enough for me!' had probably not noticed that Paul's English occasionally left something to be desired by way of lucidity let alone correct grammar. The Apostle sometimes begins to state an argument in measured language, then he expands his exposition into an elaborate analogy; his imagination soars and he gets tangled up in all kinds of inconsistencies. He stops, then starts again, often in mid-sentence. The result is a grammarian's nightmare—not because Paul was an ignorant man but more likely because he was 'in the Spirit on the Lord's Day', struggling to avoid being disobedient to the heavenly vision by reducing it to a series of cold syllogisms.

Nevertheless, the preacher has a certain freedom denied to the writer. If his message requires immediacy and directness, he can cock a snoot at *Fowler's Modern English Usage*, invent words which have never graced the pages of the *Oxford English Dictionary* and leave the subject of his sentence hanging in mid-air, mourning the loss of its object. He can rampage through the English language like an angry elephant provided, always provided, he burns with the desire to warm the hearts and enlighten the minds of his hearers by the fire of the Spirit and the reflection of the ineffable glory of God.

Despite my contention that the preacher is always subject to the laws of God but there are times when he can sit lightly to the laws of grammar, I am not suggesting that slip-shod English is self-justifying because it emanates from the pulpit. *Nothing* excuses slip-shod English, though circumstances may dictate a somewhat quixotic use of it. I reverence the English language, I love words, and if I deserve any epitaph I hope it might contain De Quincey's criticism of Coleridge: 'He never finished anything but his sentences.' There is a hidden compliment in that jibe. I would settle for *one* sentence, balanced, vivid, lucid, denuded of every superfluous word, which says something about God that may have been said a thousand times before, but never *that* way, my way, the essence of my experience, the tally of my life's quest. I doubt I could do it, but if I succeeded then all my concern for structure would be satisfied. Dr J. H. Jowett believed that *every* sermon should be capable of summary in one sentence:

> I have a conviction that no sermon is ready for preaching, nor ready for writing out, until we can express its theme in a short, pregnant sentence as clear as crystal. To compel oneself to fashion that sentence, to dismiss every word that is vague, ragged, ambiguous, to think oneself through to a form of words which defines with scrupulous exactitude—this

is surely one of the most vital and essential factors in the making of a sermon. . . .[3]

An admirable ideal, but I question whether it is capable of fulfilment in every case without limiting the range and style of preaching. The sentence that I seek and which eludes me like the Philosopher's Stone is not fashioned in the preacher's study, the first stage in sermon preparation, but evolves in the pulpit, the preacher's ultimate achievement.

However, what right have I to impose my secret ambitions on the general public, or at least, why should they pay good money to read about them? So back to the bench! What are the key differences between spoken and written words?

The first is *economy*. Inessential words may be permitted to the writer who wishes to clothe his creation in rich brocade—the fulsome adjective, the subordinate clause which adds an extra dash of colour. Style and content are inextricably interwoven in prose. But what God has joined together in one context may have to be torn apart in another. Any word which adds nothing to the clear exposition of an idea is a hindrance to speech in the service of truth. A reader can scan a sentence and if he so chooses extract the guts of it and discard the rest. To a listener, on the other hand, verbosity is a source of confusion. He discerns a diamond glinting in the flow of sludge, but before he can rescue it, the stream of words has rushed on. And what he has failed to collect in his bucket is washed away for ever. Hence, the sifting process must take place in the preacher's study and not in the congregational pew if the disproportion between what is said and what is heard is to be as small as possible.

The second is *euphony*—words which sound well together; and this, not primarily for effect but for the more utilitarian reason that the human tongue is a less flexible instrument than the pen or typewriter. The unit of spoken speech is

[3] J. H. Jowett, *The Preacher: His Life and Work*, p. 131 (New York, 1912)

neither a single word nor a complete sentence but the phrase, and it must be a phrase the preacher can pronounce with ease. There are certain combinations of words which can live together on the printed page but must be divorced if they are to trip off the preacher's tongue without tying it in knots. He might also try making a little music. Unless he is a born orator, the symphony may be beyond him but he should be able to manage a modest tune. Occasionally it is necessary to use dissonance deliberately to jar a congregation into attention, but the preacher ought not to make a habit of it. There is enough noise in the world without adding to it gratuitously.

The third is *sensuousness*—words which tease the senses, creating impressions in the mind as specific as a distinctive taste, an evocative smell or a verbal picture. Abstract generalities besides being downright dull, tempt the preach to launch a sermon before he has given sufficient time to its design to ensure its seaworthiness. Insipid, colourless concepts may span the universe in their range but unless they touch down in the hearer's backyard are unlikely to be of much practical help to him. Whenever there is fog about, the preacher has the duty of making sure it has not wafted out of the open windows of his study.

The fourth is *strength*, by which I do not mean the delivery of the sermon at the top of one's voice. Bombast is not oratory. But whenever appropriate, nouns should be concrete rather than abstract and verbs active rather than passive. My own besetting weakness is for a surfeit of adjectives and adverbs, so I hereby remind myself that they do not convey thought; they can only colour it.[4] And it is a worthless exercise trying to prop up a weak noun with a scaffolding of robust adjectives; nor does a lazy verb move any faster because it is egged on by breathless adverbs. The same is not necessarily true of the written word where it is

[4] H. G. Davis, *Design for Preaching*, p. 273 (Fortress Press, 1958)

the reader who determines the speed at which he will travel. But nothing short of a gag or an electric shock can alter the preacher's pace.

One final point. There is no punctuation in spoken speech.[5] What one preacher may deliver sonorously in a single flowing passage if he should be a devotee of the grand style, another will fire at his congregation in a series of staccato bursts. It is not the shape of the passage on the sermon manuscript which determines the rhythm of the preacher's delivery so much as the capacity of his lungs, the nature of the occasion or possibly his quirks of temperament. Those who commit their sermons to paper would be wise to bear this in mind, otherwise they will find themselves so far ahead of or behind the manuscript that they end up doing the pulpit-shuffle—juggling their papers about like an incompetent conjurer.

If one after-thought may be permitted me—I would steal from John Oman a stanza of William Cowper:

> He that negotiates between God and man,
> As God's ambassador, the grand concerns
> Of judgement and mercy, should beware
> Of lightness in his speech.[6]

Whether the preacher uses the language of the court of King James or the slang of the day, if he forfeits dignity, any other gain is illusory. The structured word has a seriousness fitted to its high purpose which any legitimate wit or playfulness can only highlight but never destroy.

2 *The Spontaneous Word*

The preacher is a human being and not a gramophone record. He would have to subscribe to the most rigorous

[5] Ibid. I have found this work most helpful on the subject of the spoken word.

[6] Quoted by J. Oman, *Concerning the Ministry* (John Knox Press, 1963)

doctrine of predestination to believe that a given sermon was foreordained from the beginning of the world to be preached on a particular occasion, come hell or high water. Nor ought his sermon to be so tightly knit that there are no crevices through which the Holy Spirit might gain entry. In fact, a sermon leaves the preacher's desk as a structure of ideas and within the setting of worship becomes an organism. Having been built, it then grows. The two images are not mutually exclusive. They are complementary. All higher forms of life have both bone and tissue, a stark skeleton as well as a complex network of pulsating cells. No preacher ought to discount the possibility that he might be possessed, taken over and carried off in an unexpected direction. There is, of course, not only Divine indwelling but also spirit-possession. He must be on his guard for evidence of either. In a fallen world, it is necessary to take seriously the ambiguous consequences of all our actions. Good intentions do not produce unequivocally good results. The human mind is hospitable to all kinds of strange and daring ideas, some inspired, others destructive, and a preacher in the pulpit, highly-strung and quivering like an athlete awaiting the starting pistol, may well blurt them out before he has been able to test them for what they are worth.

Yet granted the dangers inherent in spontaneity, it is an essential part of the creative process, transforming carefully prepared words into *the* Word for that occasion. If the unexpected cannot happen in the pulpit, it cannot happen anywhere; as Luther said, 'Let no preacher give up the faith that God wants to do a deed through him'. One of the best known illustrations of a routine, even dreary service becoming the occasion of a highly significant event concerns the conversion of Charles Haddon Spurgeon who drifted into a Methodist chapel in Colchester. There he heard a lay preacher lose the thread of his argument and in sheer desperation continue to repeat, parrot-like, his text,

'Look unto Me, and be ye saved, all the ends of the Earth'. And, as Spurgeon said afterwards, 'He had not much to say, thank God, for that compelled him to keep on reciting his text and there was nothing needed—by me, at any rate— except his text'. I doubt the poor preacher, wracking his brains throughout the previous week for some striking way of developing his text could have dreamt his utter failure would have been so powerfully used. Afterwards he probably felt he had made a fool of himself when in fact he had been a 'fool for Christ's sake'—than which there is no higher vocation.

Alexander Whyte once advised apprentice preachers: 'Let your imagination sweep up through the whole visible heavens, up to the heaven of heavens. Let her sweep and soar on her shining wing, up past sun, moon and stars.' Dr Whyte dare do it. Like all great preachers he had the power of words to make his congregations see things that are invisible, a disciplined imagination and a total lack of self-consciousness. We run-of-the-mill preachers would do well to accept the spirit of Whyte's comment but moderate the splendour of our vision to our natural capacities so that if we do get swept off our feet in the fervour of the moment we have a fighting chance of landing the right way up and not in an undignified heap at the foot of pulpit steps.

Spontaneity is not a substitute for a well-structured sermon; it is the surge which sparks its engine into life. It takes the results of our slogging preparation and injects an element of wonder so that we, along with our hearers, hear the words for the first time. And this sense of wonder is not called out by our own virtuosity but by the majesty of the truth it is our privilege to communicate. Dr Joseph Parker, who for thirty-five years reigned like a king from the pulpit of the City Temple, was a man of many quirks; his faults like his strengths were larger-than-life. But he possessed one priceless gift as a preacher. He *listened* to himself as he spoke, sharing the congregation's emotions— trepidation at his own daring, startled at his verbal thrusts, moved to tears by his word-pictures of incidents in the life of Jesus, exhilarated by his trumpet-like proclamation of the Easter Gospel. He appeared genuinely surprised at the penetrating power of the thoughts he flung like darts at his hearers. It was certainly not spur-of-the-moment preaching. His sermons were too well-shaped for that. But in spite of the hours he had spent mulling over his text, he was able to do the impossible—be in two places at once, the pulpit and the pew. He did not merely preach the Word but also heard it and so practised the dictum of the eighteenth-century Lutheran scholar, Bengel: 'Apply thyself wholly to the text; apply the matter wholly to thyself.'

Spontaneity cannot be faked; at least, it can, but only to the acute embarrassment of all who are sensitive enough to recognize crocodile tears when they see them and counterfeit passion when it is imposed on them. The more common error is less a felony than an incongruity. There are preachers who perform (and that is the appropriate word) as though they were announcing the end of the world when the *content* of their sermon makes the London telephone directory in contrast seem charged with the power of God. On the other hand there is the preacher who proclaims the imminent end of the world with all the vivacity of a radio announcer reciting vegetable prices at Covent Garden. The preacher who is incapable of being moved by the power and pathos of the Gospel is unlikely to move his hearers—except to cause a stampede the moment after he has pronounced the Benediction. Coleridge said it is a work of genius to restore what is tarnished by use to its first uncommon lustre. It is also the work of the preacher who may fall far short of genius but he has the advantage of being able to substitute personal testimony for brilliance in putting new life into old texts and religious phrases worn so smooth by constant usage that they slip down their hearers' gullets without touching their taste-buds.

A number of factors are necessary to create spontaneity— if that is not a contradiction in terms. The first is the need for the preacher to remain himself in the pulpit. Fruity elocution, unctuous mannerisms, false fervour—in short, all that is meant by 'preachyness' is more than a harmless charade. There is a sense in which it is a denial of the Incarnation. The Word which became Man is mediated from a man to men, and if it is to live it must be a man who has continuing existence outside the pulpit. He who greets people in the name of the Lord on Sunday ought not to sound or look or be any different from the one who greets them in the name of a common humanity in the post office or on the streets any other day of the week. The preacher has his own story; it is not an anecdote but a history and it won't be found in any manuscript but in the lines on his face. That's what the congregation want to hear—how he got the scars through handling the fire of God to cauterize the wounds of the world.

George Bernanos, the French author who wrote *The Diary of a Country Priest* and much else of spiritual worth besides, left behind him when he died notes for an address to be given to students at Princeton University. They contain this passage:

The priest who descends from the pulpit of Truth, with a mouth like a hen's vent, a little hot but pleased with himself, he's not been preaching: at best he's been purring like a tabby-cat. Mind you that can happen to us all, we're all half asleep, it's the devil to wake us up sometimes—the apostles slept all night at Gethsemane. Still, there's a difference . . . and mind you many a fellow who waves his arms and sweats like a furniture-remover isn't necessarily any more awakened than the rest. On the contrary, I simply mean that when the

Lord has drawn from me some word for the good of souls, I know, because of the pain of it.

To be oneself in the pulpit is not to assume the resplendent armour of a warrior for God. Any actor can do that. It is the limp, the bruise, the weals that prove a preacher wrestled all night with God like Jacob at Peniel. These are the seals of authenticity; not any fancy pulpit-garb or theological degrees or clever homiletical structure. Spontaneity is like the watermark on a bank-note. It demonstrates that the sermon is the preacher's own. By which I do not suggest that otherwise he might be suspected of plagiarism. It happens, but to anyone likely to read this book—perish the thought! Yet the preacher's work may be his own at the level of his mind but not hauled from the depths of his personal experience. Every 'I' he utters must be indicative of private anguish rather than professional egotism.

Spontaneity also involves a paradox. The preacher should be himself and yet forget himself. . . . 'I, yet not I', as Paul put it. The preacher may know his people like the back of his hand, but time has not stood still whilst he has been preparing his sermon. The congregation have had their tragedies and triumphs; they have been hurt or healed; their faith has flickered or flamed; their week has been a joy or a drag. That neat and carefully sculpted sermon structure is aimed at identi-kit man, an abstraction; a doll or a dummy rather than some real, flesh and blood person whom life has battered or blessed all the while the preacher toiled away in his study. Hence, as he looks his congregation in the eye, whole passages of rococo rhetoric will turn to dust and ashes in his mouth as he sees here and there scattered throughout the church men and women whose worry, suffering or dejection is apparent in their very posture. They are hoping against hope to receive not a cascade of oratory but a drop of mercy. This, by the way, is why the preacher should engage his congregation eye-ball to eye-ball rather than preach with eyes tight shut in mystical contemplation or gaze at the ceiling as though looking for cracks in the plaster.

The preacher must always have the courage to tear his manuscript or notes into a thousand pieces, metaphorically speaking, if circumstances demand it, and put his faith in God to haul him out of the vacuum thus created. The result may not be elegant—spontaneous speech rarely is, except for the favoured few who could not express themselves badly if their lives depended on it—but it is more important to move the stone at the mouth of the sepulchre in which someone is imprisoned than to decorate it with pretty words. And if he is a preacher of some reputation, he must shrug off the blow to his pride reflected in the disappointment of those who have come expecting great oratory. For what does his reputation matter as a weaver of cunning words compared with the good he may have done for someone who has felt a healing touch, heard a forgiving word, received the strength to live again? In short, a preacher must live with real people if he is to know their problems and he had better live with God if he is to solve them.

This is the terror of true preaching—the ever-present possibility that the preacher having spent himself in preparing the right sermon for the wrong occasion, may have to scrap it and face the people naked and defenceless. Then they will know what he is worth. All the shelves of textbooks in the theological libraries, the piles of concordances, the mountains of collected sermons will be no help to him then. He can only speak of what he knows—not out of his head but in his heart. Little wonder that St Cyran confessed that he would rather say a hundred masses than preach one sermon or that Luther said, 'Although I am old and experienced in speaking, I tremble whenever I ascend the pulpit'.

The surgeon who lacks the courage to make an incision of truly heroic length and depth if his patient's life depends upon it has no right to be in an operating theatre. By the same token, any preacher who is too timid to take a carving knife to his sermon in an emergency ought to get out of the pulpit and stay out. He is like the classical physicians who read out passages in Latin from medical textbooks by the bedside of patients writhing in pain. They edified themselves at the expense of other peoples' lives.

Spontaneity and extemporaneousness—the very length of the words is intimidating!—are two quite different qualities. The former brings immediacy to a carefully prepared sermon; the latter is speech without any formal preparation. They merge into one when the accidents of the occasion render a structured theme inappropriate or incongruous. In one case, the sermon has been pounded into shape so remorselessly that it is in danger of boring the preacher long before it gets the chance to bore the congregation—hence the need for spontaneity, a rediscovery of the life-source in it. In the other case, the sermon, so it is alleged, springs fully formed from the preacher's head, and like many premature births runs the risk of expiring for lack of maturity in all its essential parts. But what both methods have in common is the preacher's need for fluency.

It cannot be too frequently stated that the preacher must be a master of words, and there is no painless way of acquiring this skill. Admittedly, there are, in this field as any other, those who possess that quality we cannot always define but never fail to recognize—genius. Demosthenes stirring the people of Athens with his sublime Philippics; Cicero transfixing the Roman Senate; Peter the Hermit arousing the nations of Europe to embark on the Crusades; titans of the British Parliament such as Burke, Fox, Pitt, Sheridan, Gladstone, Lloyd George, Churchill, Bevan. They and their like are phenomena to be admired rather than examples to be slavishly imitated. They define the limits of what the spoken word can achieve. Their speeches are well worth reading, always provided an effort is made to bone up on our history so that their words are given a context, otherwise we may experience a sense of anti-climax. Some great orations will live for ever; others of equal power were intended for one occasion and that occasion only—read cold and in retrospect, divorced from the personality who delivered them, they are apt to disappoint. For like many good wines, oratory will not always keep. Once the bottle is opened the contents must be drunk there and then.

Nor ought one to forget that even genius extracts its price. Demosthenes, Churchill and Bevan—each had to overcome speech impediments; John Ball, the priest and supporter of Wat Tyler, whose address to the rebels at Blackheath in 1381 has secured him a place in the annals of British oratory, was semi-literate; Gladstone's famous election speech at Midlothian in 1879 is as heavy as dough and dense like suet pudding—yet on *that* occasion over-whelming in its effect; William Morris debating in Hammer-smith with George Bernard Shaw was so nervous he almost fainted, and the Churchill whose war-time speeches rallied a reeling nation could be downright dull when as a post-war Prime Minister he had to address the Commons on domestic issues which held little interest for him; Aneurin Bevan, on the other hand, could make the subject of drains as exciting as Churchill's encomium on the Few to whom so many owed so much—yet the Welsh socialist's voice was high-pitched to the point of squeakiness. So let the ordinary preacher be of good cheer. Even the greatest had their handicaps.

What, then is the key to fluency? The enlargement of vocabulary comes from constant reading, not simply to add to the number of uncommon words in one's armoury but to study how powerful ideas are fleshed out in language; to learn the cadences of sentences; to puzzle out why a master of English chooses a particular word and not half a dozen others which apparently mean the same thing but are as little at home in *that* context as a publican at a Band of Hope Meeting. Many great speakers and writers had their favourite authors, over whose works they pored hour after hour. Cardinal Newman was an Athanasius-addict; John Bunyan read Luther's writings over and over again, and he in turn was Alexander Whyte's great love; Gladstone wrestled with the philosophical prose of Bishop Butler; the younger Pitt imbibed Demosthenes with his mother's milk; uncharacteristically, the Scottish theologian, Dr Marcus Dods steeped himself in the writings of the Anglo-Catholic, F. W. Faber.

I blush to add myself, even as an appendix (and we all know what a useless organ that is!) to such distinguished company. But every dog has his day. My spoken style is owed in the main to two late Victorian writers as dissimilar as chalk and cheese—G. K. Chesterton, the genie of the sparkling epigram, and Charles Dickens who used the language of the people to paint unforgettable word-pictures. And because every self-respecting parson is expected to own allegiance to some great theologian, I choose Reinhold Niebhur who, in such works as *Beyond Tragedy* showed how it is possible to be both profound and yet intelligible to inferior minds.

The modern preacher is likely to pass by the great classics with a respectful nod of the head and choose some work which uses the idiom of our day. So be it. So long as he picks authors *who have something to say*, even though he may not personally agree with all or any of it, then they will have served their purpose. For he is training himself not to be garrulous—there's many a self-taught master of that around —but to use and handle words with the skill and familiarity an artist uses brushes and paint.

Let every apprentice-preacher identify in the heavens his own lode-star and sit at the feet of whoever it hovers over, whether politician, preacher, novelist or pamphleteer. Read,

read, read! Then analyse what has been read to ferret out the secret of its power and lucidity. There is no other way to be sure that appropriate words are on call when needed.

I end with a paradox. Sermon-structure is the work of a few hours: spontaneity is the fruit of a life-time's labour. And neither without the other has the power to lodge a truth of God in the hearer's mind. Spontaneity without structure is life without form. Structure without spontaneity is form without life. Only in conjunction do they constitute authentic preaching. The Word becomes flesh, but more important, it lives.

EIGHT

The Word—Silent yet Active

1 *The Silent Word*

To talk about the silent Word seems a contradiction in terms. We tend to regard speech as a chain of words, broken only by the demands of punctuation or the need to draw breath. In fact, the space between words—silence—is as much a part of communication as what is actually said. Confucius likened language to a wheel. The spokes hold the structure together, they are the syntax if you like, but the empty spaces in between convey the essence of what is said. And the ear recognizes that this is so even if the written word takes no account of the fact. Listen to an everyday conversation. Each speaker does not pour out words in a continual flow until interrupted or answered by the other. There are pauses, hesitations, false starts, hummings and hawings. These apparent solecisms are an integral part of the communication process. They convey not merely the atmosphere or mood of the occasion but are indicators of the quality of relationship between speaker and listener.

Ivan Illich, writing about the problem of getting Spanish-speaking Puerto-Rican immigrants and native New Yorkers to overcome the language barrier so that they can understand one another, puts great store on silence as a form of communication—not the silence of boredom or indifference, but of keen interest and close attention. And he asserts that it is not the other man's words but his silences we must interpret if there is to be genuine contact. Says Illich, 'The learning of the grammar of silence is an art much more difficult to learn than the grammar of sounds.'

Many linguists would support Illich's contention that more is relayed from person to person through pauses and hesitations than by the agency of words. Indeed, Illich, former Catholic priest and formidable critic of many of society's most cherished assumptions adds a theological dimension to this view of communication:

> As words must be learned by listening and painful attempts at imitation of a native speaker, so silences must be acquired by a delicate openness to them. Silence has its pauses and hesitations; its rhythms and expressions and inflections; its durations and pitches, and times to be and not to be. Just as with our words, there is an analogy between our silence with men and with God. To learn the full meaning of one, we must practise and deepen the other. . . .[1]

It is vital that the preacher understands the nature of silence as an essential element in the communication process. And such understanding does not come easily to pulpiteers, of all people, because they are inveterate talkers. Indeed, Christians in general have become so accustomed to treating the world as a captive audience that we have virtually abandoned the ministry of listening. Whenever there is silence, we feel in honour-bound to fill it with wodges of God-talk. Protestants in particular would not make good Trappist monks, professing vows of perpetual silence. We even find structured silence—meditation—uncongenial. And so fluent do we become in the use of words that it is as though they vaporize and the hearer absorbs them through his skin instead of their impinging on his consciousness.

[1] I. D. Illich, *Celebration of Awareness* (Doubleday, 1970)

138

The Word—Silent yet Active

One reason we find silence unbearable is that when we stop prating we *hear* ourselves; all the groanings of our inner disease, like the ominous creaking of a ship's bulkheads in a storm—grinding teeth, tapping fingers, the twanging of stretched nerves, silent screams of frustration or even the hollow echo of inner spiritual deadness. We are not at peace, so we drown out our internal dissonance with a torrent of words. We call it communication but it is actually a form of camouflage, hiding our self-preoccupation and lack of wholeness. A preacher's ability to come to terms with silence is one indicator of his own spiritual condition.

But how does silence figure in the preacher's pulpit technique? I am not thinking of dramatic pauses consciously contrived. They may have their effect so long as they do not smack of theatricality and provided they are used sparingly —otherwise the congregation will begin to suspect they are listening not to a preacher with great power but one with a poor memory. The relationship between words and silence is three-fold.

There is the silence *before* words. Some preachers gallop into the pulpit, whip out their notes and launch into their theme without so much as a glance at the congregation. And one has the impression that were they to look up half-way through the first sentence and discover the pews had been invaded by little green men from Mars, they wouldn't turn a hair but carry on their pre-destined course oblivious of the fact that the unusual composition of the congregation, to put it mildly, might demand some change of policy, if only to nip down, shake the leader of the contingent by whatever protuberance passed for a hand and enquire politely whether they spoke English.

This silence before speech has certain parallels in the counselling situation. Doctors, for instance, who have some degree of insight into the human personality, recognize the importance of listening with close attention to a patient's rambling recital of symptoms, often outward signs of an inner turmoil which is not physical in origin. Sometimes the patient leaves without a prescription but feeling better. He has been heard. His personhood has been acknowledged. Granted, the preacher's context is very different since he is the one about to do the talking. But the basic principle is the same. The ministry of the Word ought to be preceded by a ministry of listening. The sounds will be vague and unrelated—shuffling, the odd cough, the noise of passing traffic and so on. These apparent irrelevancies can tell the preacher much, not only about the mood and atmosphere of the congregation but possible sources of distraction. And it is the totality of what he hears and what he says which together determine the rhythm and style of his preaching. In a moment of silence, of listening, he consciously acknowledges the personhood of every member of the congregation. They are not souls with ears into which is poured saving truth like a constant stream of tea from an urn across a moving belt of empty cups.

Martin Buber[2] uses the illustration of two men sitting on a park bench, total strangers. They neither say nor do anything to establish contact, but provided the attitude of one is openness to the other, a recognition he is *there*, a miracle like the lifting of a spell takes place and communication streams from him and the silence bears it to his neighbour. A word of dialogue has happened sacramentally even though in the end neither 'knows' a single thing about the other.

Sacramental silence is an excellent way of describing this joining of speaker and hearers in one continuum before the formal sermon begins. Preacher and congregation have acknowledged that they are *there* as persons—not a disembodied voice addressing the occupants of those pews 'out there'. In a secular context, this process would be termed a

[2] Martin Buber, *Between Man and Man* (Macmillan, 1965)

speaker establishing rapport with his hearers. But when it is the Gospel with which we are concerned, there is more at stake than the natural orator's ability to get on the wavelength of his audience. Both preacher and congregation must demonstrate their openness to the Holy Spirit, which does not necessarily become a presence as a result of an invocatory prayer before the text is announced. An apposite analogy might be that of a spark of electricity jumping the gap between two electrodes. As always, the Psalmist put it better—'For God alone my soul awaits in silence.' Just as the murmur of conversation dies away when the arrival of an earthly dignitary is imminent, so a silence measured in seconds may make an eternity of difference when preacher and people are about to pay homage to the Word who is universal Lord. And some present who do not find God in the wind, earthquake and fire of a spirited sermon may hear him in that still, small voice, too subdued to break the silence which precedes it.

There is a mandatory chapter in most textbooks on preaching about the relationship between the ministry of proclamation and that of pastoral care. It is important and needs to be said. So I have said it and wish only to emphasize one aspect of the pastoral office, that of *listening*. I am not now concerned with the truth that it is an understanding of people's every day cares and joy which brings freshness and urgency to the preacher's sermons, with the necessary qualification that it is immoral to use them as sermon illustrations even though thinly disguised. Nor am I anxious to belabour the point that problems often either vanish or are reduced to their true proportions when they are articulated—though that too is sometimes the case. My contention is simply that he who does not know how to listen forfeits both the right and ability to speak. There is a dialectic between listening and talking which, however private the setting in which it takes place, has echoes in the pulpit.

As well as the silence *before* words, there is the silence *between* words. And again I am not dealing with mechanics, the pace at which the preacher delivers a sermon. That is a stylistic matter or a function of temperament. Some preachers develop their argument with the ponderous deliberation of an elephant, others scamper along like gazelles. Silence between words acknowledges the sermon as a living organism, growing rather than being built. The preacher who is tied to a *verbatim* manuscript has a particular problem. He has already constructed his sentences and though he might vary the speed of his delivery, his freedom to digress from the script is severely limited if only because any passages added on the spur of the moment may not only distort the preconceived shape of his sermon but send him off on a new tack which could either open up an entirely new field or else prove a dead end. I would affirm that whether the preacher uses a manuscript, notes or speaks extemporaneously, he must be prepared to take the risk. Otherwise he might just as well hand out to his congregation duplicated copies of his sermon. It is fixed, final and impervious to the subtle pressures of the Spirit upon him.

In ordinary conversation, silence *between* words is a gesture of respect, a symbol that he who speaks takes seriously the concerns of the hearer. By forbearing to spew out an endless stream of platitudes but painfully struggling to find the exact word, the speaker is, in that endless moment whilst he ransacks his vocabulary, engaged in the search for a common experience which lies deeper than the level of language.

Unless the sermon takes the form of a dialogue where one person's choice of words depends on what is said to him, the preacher has much less scope in searching for *the* word which bears the burden of the truth he is anxious to convey *at that moment*. Even so, he would be wise not to imprison himself in a strait-jacket of pre-packaged language, for he is, after all, dealing in mystery. And if he has no sense that he is encroaching upon this area of mystery, or possibly worse, trying to articulate with precision its dimensions, he is like a child playing with marbles whilst a cataclysmic event takes place around him.

There are no words for our deepest experiences—communion between lovers, awe in the presence of death, horror at a scene of widespread devastation such as flood, famine or earthquake. What can be said which does not diminish or trivialize the truth? In a sense, preaching does the same to God, however devout or eloquent the person in the pulpit—which is why I claimed earlier that preaching is not difficult but strictly impossible. Nevertheless, silence between words, especially those that form part of the traditional vocabulary of the Christian faith—which many people would assert are antiquated—might have a two-fold value—symbolize the preacher's awareness that he is struggling with the inexpressible and also allow mystery itself to break out of its linguistic prison—God repudiating our petty images of him and speaking for himself in the language of silence: no new insight, this, the Quakers have known and practised it for centuries.

But I must emphasize yet again that silence as an integral part of sermon structure is not a matter of style, a theatrical gesture. It must be born out of the preacher's genuine awareness of a mystery which eludes his grasp and tantalizes his mind. Otherwise, silence will lose the dimension of bottomless depth and become simply a pause, a gap between outbursts of God-gossip.

Silence *beyond* words is closely related to silence *between* words. Again, it is easier to define in one-to-one relationships than in the public forum. It is the situation in which there is nothing more to be said. The silence beyond words may be a salute to another's courage or identification with his anguish or just an unspoken *yes* to an unformulated plea for help, understanding, forgiveness or love.

Where is the silence beyond words to be found in the sermon? The answer, surely, is that it isn't, but in the preacher's own awareness that he is not only being used but also overheard. It is an overtone of his integrity, a sense of consistency between what he proclaims publicly and practises personally. When a man professes more than he believes or uses oratorical tricks to by-pass the minds of his listeners in order to get at their emotions, the silence beyond words degenerates into a hollowness within them. Richard Baxter, the seventeenth-century divine, vividly described the way a preacher's quality of life negates or increases the force of his words:

> Many a tailor goes in rags that maketh costly clothes for others; and many a cook scarcely licks his fingers when he hath dressed for others the most costly dishes. . . . Take heed to yourselves, lest you perish, while you call upon others to take heed of perishing! lest you famish yourselves while you prepare their food. . . .[3]

When talking about a third party in his presence, it behoves one to choose words with care. The silence beyond words may be that of Divine endorsement or Judgement. And the preacher 'hears' this silence, even though his congregation are deaf to all but what is being said. And which preacher worth his salt has not occasionally crept out of the pulpit conscious of having betrayed his integrity—any complimentary comments from his people feeling less a pat on the back than a shaft through the heart?

So the silent Word is not less efficacious because it is inaudible. And to hear it is not a skill the preacher acquires but a burden that is imposed upon him. His ear becomes attuned to it the longer he practises his craft. It is God's contribution to a dialogue with him that never ends. If he

[3] Quoted in *The Minister's Prayer Book*, p. 329 (Collins, 1964)

is a faithful servant of the Word, it is a core of inner peace however tumultuous his life; if he is not, it is the terrible aloneness of dereliction.

2 *The Active Word*

The preacher is not only a Christian orator. There are times when he is for one reason or another prevented from speaking openly of Jesus. Then the silent Word must express itself through his actions or even his bare presence within a situation as a Christian.

Contemporary Mission thrusts upon the Christian unprecedented situations which demand that if he is to make any impact at all, he must become an exponent of the silent Word. A century ago, the whole world was spread out before the Western missionary as a passive audience for the proclamation of the Gospel. The gusts of revolutionary political change have slammed shut many doors and left others only slightly ajar. There are some nations whose governments refuse entry to all Westerners, whatever their role or motivation; others will permit and even welcome Western doctors, teachers and technicians on condition they do not propagate Christianity. So the Bible's injunction to preach the Gospel to all nations has collided with hard political realities. Even the West itself, though still acknowledging the Christian tradition which did much to shape it, shows little inclination to move within range of the preacher's voice.

What form of communication is possible between a dumb preacher and deaf listeners? The silent Word of action, embodied in those who live by Jesus' injunction—'Be not speakers of the Word alone but doers of it.' John Taylor in his formative work on the Holy Spirit and the Christian Mission instances the witness of Père Charles de Foucauld and his Little Brothers and Little Sisters of Jesus, who have placed themselves under rule not to preach or employ any of the institutional outworkings of evangelism, hospitals, schools and the like. Quoting Charles de Foucauld's dictum, 'I wish to cry the gospel by my whole life!' Taylor gives examples of the silent, hidden presence of love expressed in action throughout the world by members of this Order:

> They believe they are simply called to live among the very poor of this world—on a house-boat amid the teeming refugees of Hong Kong, around a tiny courtyard high above the sacred waterfront of Banares, in a workman's shack on one of the sloping streets of Kabul, in an Eskimo hamlet in Alaska, a shanty suburb of Kampala, a labourers' settlement near Port Moresby, built on wooden piles above the sea like any other village of Papua. Unobtrusively they keep a routine of communal prayer and silent adoration, but every day go out in their working clothes to do the same sort of job as their neighbours and to offer them an unstinting friendship in the doing of it.[4]

And John Taylor comments, 'Such extreme renunciation of all the normal activities of mission would suggest either a lack of concern or a policy of despair, were it not for Charles de Foucauld's ardent passion for evangelism. . . . To live thus totally towards God for the sake of the world is a profoundly missionary and, indeed, redemptive way. But only faith can perceive this.'

If it should be charged that I have moved out of the realm of homiletics into that of Christian action then I would feel vindicated rather than guilty. I have asserted on a number of occasions that the study-bound preacher—except in certain special cases—has gone. Oratory in a vacuum vanished with the last of the pulpit titans. There is a causal relationship between Christian action and Christian proclamation which thrusts down deep roots into the Gospel itself.

[4] Taylor, *The Go-Between God* (Fortress Press, 1973)

As Jesus himself said: 'For the words that the mouth utters come from the overflowing of the heart', and 'Why do you keep calling me "Lord, Lord"—and never do what I tell you?' In the same passage, Jesus pictured talk without action as a good tree producing worthless fruit or a house built on shaky foundations. There is an authenticity and power about the witness of a man who has faced the possibility of his own death in a situation of persecution or the re-enactment of the ministry of Christ where people suffer dire need, which is preaching of the most eloquent sort though not a single word has been spoken.

The United Mission to Nepal is a good example of Christian Mission in which the silent Word can only be proclaimed in action. The King of Nepal welcomes Westerners who bring skills and knowledge of which his people are bereft. He welcomes Christians and devotees of any religion, but makes it a condition of their going that they do nothing to win over Nepalis from their ancestral faith to another. Indeed, it is a criminal offence for a Nepali to become a Christian unless that is the faith of his parents. Hence, preaching is out. Understandably, there was heated debate amongst Western missionary leaders as to whether they could accept such stringent limitations upon their freedom to preach the Gospel and make Christians 'from the nations'. In the end, the United Mission to Nepal was established, supported by many missionary societies and movements, which sent in doctors, teachers, engineers and other technicians who were Christians but not professional evangelists. It was an act of faith in the power of Jesus to make himself known when Christians do his deeds. Here is anonymous ministry and silent proclamation—the wordless re-enactment of Christ's Passion.

Just as God's existence is not predicated upon our proclamation of him so the resurrection power of Jesus is at work in a world where no formal acknowledgement of it is possible. Teilhard de Chardin gives us a clue about the power of *belief* to transform unregenerate Creation:

> Though the phenomena of the lower world remain the same—the material determinations, the vicissitudes of chance, the laws of labour, the agitations of men, the footfalls of death—he who dares to believe reaches a sphere of created reality in which all things, whilst retaining their habitual texture, seem to be made out of a different substance. Everything remains the same so far as phenomena are concerned, but at the same time, everything becomes luminous, animated, loving. . . .[5]

Possibly silent witnesses to Christ project a vision which other men see and long to make their own. Perhaps we can extend the scope of the statement in the Epistle of James that 'we know we have passed out of death into life, because we love the brethren' by having faith that the brethren too also pass from death to life because we show our love for them in any way we can.

I make no pretensions to understanding the mechanics of silent proclamation through service. It is in the hands of God, which is no bad thing when we have studied preaching from this angle and that until it has virtually become a science. Here we are *really* out of our depth and can only profess an agnosticism enlivened by hope.

The activity of the silent Word reaches its paradoxical climax in those situations in which there is neither Christian speech nor action but simply presence. Ralph Harper, to whose book, *The Sleeping Beauty*, John Taylor first drew my attention, contrasts all the well-intentioned jabbering and chatter of Christians, their business and organization, their frenetic activity for God's sake, with the face-to-face character of true presence which flourishes in silence:

> Each order of experience has its own atmosphere. The atmosphere of presence, of giving, of wholeness, is silence.

[5] Quoted by Appleton, *Journey for a Soul*, p. 213 (Collins, 1974)

We know that serious things have to be done in silence, because we do not have words to measure the immeasurable. In silence, men love, pray, listen, paint, write, think, suffer. These experiences are all occasions of giving and receiving, of some encounter with forces that are inexhaustible and independent of us. These are easily distinguishable from our routines and possessiveness as silence is distinct from noise.[6]

Presence is an infinitely richer state than shared existence. For we can rub shoulders with our fellowmen, even spend our lives with them and still be insensitive to the mystery of the other which is a reflection of the mystery of God in whose image we are made. Presence involves openness, vulnerability, self-offering. There is no attempt to manipulate the other, even to manoeuvre him into the Kingdom. Compassion—'suffering with'—is the active state of presence. 'He who suffers is God's representative', wrote a Hindu poet; one might add that he who shares that suffering is equally God's representative. The condition for Christian presence is that one should be whole, at peace, devoid of inner turmoil—all that might inhibit the free flow of God's love and truth through one personality to another.

If compassion is one condition of Christian presence, a willingness to be guided is another. Inner dialogue between God and his servants does not cease when they abandon their public roles as speakers and activists on his behalf and become private persons. They are addressed from a realm beyond themselves and entrusted with a gift which they are bound to care for loyally. That gift is often a tiny share of God's suffering love for men, a twinge of his anxiety for their welfare, a flash of the truth he wants them to receive. True Christian presence means, therefore, an exact sense of priorities—not only acceptance of God's gift but the willingness to deliver it to its destination at the expense of

[6] Harper, *The Sleeping Beauty*, p. 111 (Harvill, 1956)

all contingent commitments, carefully laid plans, and crowded diaries.

What has all this to do with preaching? Nothing and yet everything. God's silent but active Word both warns the preacher that he is expendable and delivers him from the fret and worry that he might fall short of his high vocation. He can lose his voice, be turned out of his pulpit, banned from preaching the Gospel, cut off from the people of God, imprisoned, laid aside by sickness, and yet . . . so long as he draws breath, the God of infinite initiatives will find some way of using him. Dr W. E. Sangster, one of the great Methodist preachers of this century, in the flood-tide of his power, delivered many superb sermons, but there are those who will testify that he was most eloquent when, almost totally paralyzed, he could barely lift a finger to communicate with those who came to visit him. They went to comfort him and left instead with their faith renewed. So speaks the silent Word.

NINE

The Word—Decisive and Final

1 *The Decisive Word*

To begin with a resounding cliché—Christianity is an historical religion. Possibly it loses something as a result, at least so far as the embroidery is concerned. We boast no pantheon of mythical gods, around whose doings have grown up stories of great lyrical beauty. Both Greek and Roman mythology have given us a body of literature which has enriched the world. And the Northern European tradition, more austere to match the rigours of the climate in which it was nourished, inspired composers such as Wagner, Grieg and Sibelius to produce mighty music. Eastern religions have added poetry, vision and fire to Mankind's spiritual treasure-trove. Christianity involves a complex interplay of mystical detachment and social involvement, superbly illustrated by the story of Israel; but at its heart are a finite number of facts which together comprise the Jesus-Event. And we cannot stray far from these facts without perpetrating grave heresy or even founding a new religion.

C. H. Dodd in a slender book whose importance is totally out of proportion to its size, *The Apostolic Preaching and its Developments* (Hodder, 1936), has distilled the essence of the Gospel of the primitive Church into a series of deceptively simple statements. In sum: the age of fulfilment for which the people of Israel longed and prayed and suffered has dawned because of the Jesus-Event—his life, teaching, works, death, resurrection and ascension; this same Jesus is the head of the New Israel, enthroned at God's right hand; the gift of the Spirit is the sign of Christ's continuing presence within history which will be consummated by his return in Glory to make manifest what is now latent—his Lordship over a new Creation—and the response God requires of those who desire to enter into this new life, eternal in quality, is repentance and faith.

That's it—the Christian Faith in a nut-shell. That is all which needs to be said. But it is important to note that *all* of it needs to be said. The Gospel may consist of a finite number of facts, but any true preaching requires that none should be emphasized at the expense of others. Many of the Church's tragic divisions have been caused by zealous Christians who, believing that a doctrine was suffering neglect, proceeded to exalt it, generally to the exclusion of others. The constant harping of some Evangelicals upon the Cross; the insistence of theological liberals upon reducing the Gospel to a social and political ideology; the massive emphasis of the Pentecostals on the Holy Spirit; the abandonment of historical responsibility by the Seventh Day Adventists for a faith centred in the imminence of the Second Coming—for the worthiest of reasons, the wholeness of the Gospel has been torn apart.

The Gospel consists of facts, and the true preaching of it requires that the totality of the Jesus-Event should be set forth. Too many pulpiteers are masters of the one-string fiddle, and a marvellous variety of tunes they can play, but it is not the fully orchestrated music of Redemption. The Church's liturgical year has the advantage that it ensures no aspect of the Jesus-Event is forgotten, so the preacher would do well to take account of it. But he ought not to allow it to become a strait-jacket or even worse, a set of pigeon-holes into which great doctrines are popped and left to wait until they are taken out, dusted and preached again at the appropriate season of the following year.

My own experience has taught me just how unadventurous I am. I cannot recall preaching a Christmas sermon at the height of the summer, and I suspect my congregation would think I was suffering from mental confusion if I did. Pentecost in autumn, Ascension in the bleak mid-winter? Why not? Are not these great verities universally relevant? Certainly they ought not to be subject to the tyranny of the calendar. Indeed, they might gain in freshness and drive deeper into the consciousness of the congregation if they were transmitted out of phase, as it were. Granted, the organist might find an Order of Service built round Christmas carols startling on August Bank holiday Sunday. But then, organists develop their own defence-mechanism for coping with the vagaries of preachers.

Equally important is the need for the preacher to recognize the versatility of basic Christian doctrines. If he is hell-bent on conversions (speaking ironically of course) why should he assume that the Cross is the mandatory sermon theme? Has not the Resurrection redemptive power? The Christian activist might profitably give more attention to what is unbiblically described as the Second Coming. Divested of its more garish imagery, the doctrine has profound political consequences—as the expositors of the so-called Theology of Hope such as Moltmann, Metz, Bloch, Pannenberg and Alves have discovered at a more technical level. And John Robinson—not the Puritan, the bishop—has, by transliterating *Ascension* into *Ascendancy*, laid bare a rich vein of gold for the preacher who seeks to be prophetic about events of our time.

So the facts upon which the Christian Faith rests may be

finite in number, but the permutations and combinations, expressed in terms of doctrines set within personal and corporate contexts provide the almost endless variety of preaching themes. So let the preacher take an axe to the pigeon-holes and allow the Gospel to run free. Turn the Christian year upside down and inside out if need be, and give the Spirit its sway. The only cautionary note to be sounded is that the limits of Christian advocacy are those set by the Bible and not by the exercise of sanctified imagination on the part of a preacher who is determined to be different at any price. He would do well to bear in mind the closing words of John's Gospel: 'There is much else that Jesus did. If it were all to be recorded in detail, I suppose the whole world could not hold the books that would be written'—or one might add, the sermons that have been preached. It is, therefore, unlikely that some pristine truth of Christianity which has lain dormant for two thousand years will suddenly take up residence in the preacher's mind so that he can unleash it on a startled world.

To take the argument a stage further—the facts upon which the Gospel are based are of a special kind. They are *decisive* facts. They demand some response from the hearer. There are some facts I can take or leave according to my interests or temperament. I find it difficult to get het up about the fact that the Planet Uranus has a mean distance from the Sun of 1,783 million miles. Nor do Lambert's conformal conic projections set my heart pounding with excitement. And I doubt my life would be permanently impoverished if Dickens' last and unfinished novel, *The Mystery of Edwin Drood* remained unsolved. But there are facts, neutral in character, which can become decisive, in the sense that I am required to do something about them, should circumstances change. The comment, 'I hear the River Thames flows at the bottom of your garden' is likely to elicit a polite response, whereas the warning, 'That river at the bottom of your garden has overflowed its banks!' will set me off at a gallop.

Thus we come to the crunch of preaching. When we have defined, dissected and analysed it every which way, the central function of preaching is to make Christians by confronting people with the claims of Jesus. The sermon may be an act of adoration, a method of teaching by exposition, but at its heart there must be thrusting challenge, the articulation of God's imperious demand, the offer of his forgiveness and the gift of his grace.

The phrase 'to preach for a verdict' has become common coinage in the vocabulary of homiletics. It is not, I think, a happy one, though the general idea is sound. There is about it the smack of the argumentative, the overtones of the forensic. It is a litigious phrase. One can win a verdict by sheer brilliance, outright lying, twisting the law or appealing to unworthy motives. A verdict need not be derived from the facts and anyway, is aimed at a third party—Judge, jury or tribunal. But taking into account all these qualifications, the phrase does remind the preacher that he is not in the pulpit to entertain his hearers or divert them with an interesting discourse of some kind. The analogy with a barrister should remind him that he is about a deadly business. A case half-prepared, lackadaisical presentation of the facts and the course of a client's whole life might be adversely changed.

We would do better to follow the example of Jesus and find our illustrations from within Nature rather than the courts. The tragedy of much modern preaching is that we fail to reap the harvest we have sown. The mature wheat is allowed to remain in the field and rot. The reasons are various. Some preachers think it immoral to subject individuals to what might be called the psychic or spiritual pressure of appeal for personal response. They scorn what they believe to be emotional manipulation—as though the emotions are not an integral part of the human personality! Others subscribe to a doctrine of the Church which leads them to an understanding of preaching as raising the corporate spiritual temperature of the whole congregation rather than singling out individuals. Still more are sensitive to the possibility that they might be regarded as pocketsized Billy Grahams. And here, intellectual snobbery rears its sleek head. Mass evangelists, especially of Graham ilk tend to embarrass congregations. There seems to be too much razmataz, too little theological content and a Gospel which touches the pressure-points of life only incidentally. They may or may not be right, but what cannot be denied is that when they have finished demolishing Billy Graham on every conceivable ground, the challenge remains. Why is it that people who have sat under our preaching for years without any noticeable effect, come alive in a quite new way when the claims of Jesus upon men are put in a way which invites them to stand up and be counted?

Paradoxically, it could be argued that we preachers are reaping exactly what we have sown—a thin Gospel producing a sparse harvest. Whole areas of the modern Church seem to be modelled upon that of Laodicia—neither hot nor cold and therefore spewed out of the mouth of God. We are victims of our gospel of the minimal demand. We plead that our people might spare us the odd half-hour out of their crowded diaries. Tithing is unacceptable so we beg the odd twenty pence. People are easily bored so we promise them a ten-minute address in place of a full-blown sermon. We do not ask for sacrifice but assure them that they will suffer only slight inconvenience should they be willing to take up office in the Church.

Let us be brutally frank: one reason why we of the older generation have forfeited the respect of the young is not that we have made too many demands upon them but too few. They are bursting with idealism; they want to give themselves to a cause which enlists every fibre of their being. Political movements such as nationalism and communism which make life or death demands upon their followers, are never short of volunteers. It is one of the quirks of human nature that people who would not offer you a few pence for a good cause will write a cheque for a thousand pounds. They judge the value of an appeal by the size of the demand we make upon them. So it is with our preaching. Ask congregations for the odd hour of their time in the service of the Kingdom and they will plead pressure of work or family commitments or other engagements of a socially beneficial kind. Demand everything in the name of Jesus and you have a fighting chance of getting it.

A minister once complained to Charles Haddon Spurgeon about the small number of conversions which resulted from his preaching. Spurgeon replied, 'Surely you don't expect conversions from every sermon, do you?' 'Certainly not!' replied the preacher; to which Spurgeon retorted, 'Then if you do not expect them, you will not have them.' The famous Victorian preacher had unerringly uncovered the blight of modern preaching—small expectation. We get what we ask for: decency, social morality, political awareness, regular church-going. Ask, and it will be given unto you. But if you do not demand total commitment, spiritual revolution, re-assessment of one's priorities to bring them into line with those of Jesus, then what right have you to expect them?

There was a legendary Dr Finney in the United States at the turn of the century who was something of a martinet. He startled his deacons in the vestry before Service on one occasion by concluding his prayer by drawing the Almighty's attention to the large number of non-believers who had been attracted by his oratory to hear him, pleaded for their conversion, adding, '. . . and thou knowest, Lord, that in these matters I am not accustomed to being denied.' Whatever may be thought of the theology or even propriety of such an attitude, it is a matter of history that Dr Finney's preaching had much success—in the worthiest sense of the word. A man of such large expectations is unlikely to be disappointed. By the same token, modern preachers rarely approach the pulpit with a philosophy of the sermon based on Ruskin's definition—'thirty minutes to raise the dead.' Little wonder the spiritually moribund scarcely stir from their catatonic state let alone emerge like Lazarus from the tomb, trailing their linen wrappings behind them!

So the Word is embodied within a number of decisive facts and it is the preacher's duty to beseech men in Christ's name to make some response to them. This means that the preacher, whatever his churchmanship, theological complexion and life-situation is an evangelist. He may well be many other things as well, but this one thing he must be. Which brings us to a subject from which the modern Church in whole areas of its life coyly retreats. Let me make my own position crystal clear. I have probably been as involved in the political life of a nation as most ministers; I have used my pulpit during Zambia's freedom struggle to speak out against the evils of colonialism and racial discrimination. I still believe that the preacher by the power of the Gospel is an agent of radical political change. I am a disciple of Reinhold Niebhur and limp along a good way behind him, utterly sure that as the years wear on he will be recognized as having wrestled longer and more successfully with the key issues of our time than any other theologian I have read. Yet I would still lay claim to the title of evangelist and see my most important task as a preacher in introducing men to their Lord.

So I believe that the Church which does not believe in conversion is faithless and the preacher who does not demand a personal response to the Gospel has no place in the pulpit. But by *conversion* I do not mean taking men and women out of the work-a-day world and vaporizing them, so that they become exponents of superheated pietism, full of prayer and praise but unavailable for service in the battle-line where the struggle for a better society is taking place. In my view, conversion does not mean adding an extra dimension—the religious—to all other dimensions of our existence, but the unsnarling of the tangled threads of our lives so that, by an act of will, we bring our priorities into line with those of Jesus and derive the power for living from the same source as that from which Jesus drew his.

Hence, when someone approaches me with the light of religious fervour in his eyes and assures me joyously that he has been converted, I do not want to know what effect this experience has had upon his churchgoing or prayer-life, but how it has manifested itself at the pressure-points of his life—in his attitudes to sex, money, ambition, power, race, politics. John Vincent has put it well:

> Evangelism has as its aim Discipleship. Evangelism is the presentation of life and word of the radical offer and demand of God. This offer and demand is never abstract or 'spiritual', but is always a demand for a particular response in a particular situation. To say, 'Yes' to Christ is always to say 'Yes' to a particular deed of Christ in the world. Faithful evangelism attempts to depict the crucial incarnateness of the Word: crucial because the only word of God we can know is his word in the cross, incarnateness because the only word of God we can know is his Word made flesh and dwelling amongst us. 'Decision' becomes decision about present, actual, real-life issues, not about some vague, temporary attitude of the heart. 'Conversion' becomes conversion not as a momentary change of heart, but as a complete reversal of motivation, vocation, life and action.[1]

Just as modern missionary societies are having to come to terms with the candidate who makes no profession to a

[1] J. J. Vincent, *Christ and Methodism* (Abingdon Press, 1965)

life-time commitment to service overseas, but is willing to make a conditional offer—one tour beyond which he has no clear idea of what God wishes to do with him, so the conversion which is a Damascus road experience—total, irrevocable change of life-style—is giving place to an understanding of conversion as offering a small part of one's life to God, with the expectation that the rest will follow in due time. Of course, redemption is transformation of the whole person, but it must begin *somewhere*, and the preacher who gets one single member of his congregation to rid himself of racial prejudice, for instance, is not proclaiming some social Gospel; he has started someone on the road to a radical change of life-style. This is evangelism. When Jesus invited men to follow him, he took them as they were in particular life-situations and forced upon them hard decisions. He did not envelop them in a pink cloud of religiosity which dealt with the rough, tough business of life by wafting them above it. He never showed them a way *out* of their problems, but offered them a way *through* them. And invariably as they fought their way forward, they found a cross and a tomb barring their way, an experience of sacrificial death and glorious resurrection to be faced and suffered but with the assurance of renewal, for Jesus asks nothing of us that he himself has not undergone.

We often hear talk about Art for Art's sake or Sport for Sport's sake, but there is no such thing as Preaching for Preaching's sake—or at least there is, but there oughtn't to be. Preaching can never be a self-justifying art; the preacher always has an ulterior motive. Structure, vocabulary, ideas are like the moving parts of an engine. They are not linked together in order to create a pretty object but to *drive* something, to change someone. I may be pessimistic, but I very much doubt that the average churchgoer sets off for Service with a sense of anticipation tinged with apprehension because the whole course of his life may be altered as a result of something that is said, sung or done during worship. I am probably doing my fellow-preachers a grave injustice, but I wonder how many would know what to say or do if a member of the congregation got to his feet at the end of the Service and announced that his half-hearted conviction had been transformed into full-blooded conversion and what ought he to do next? Embarrassment, astonishment, even uneasiness, but expectation, preparedness, quiet confidence? I wonder.

The decisive facts of the Gospel have their own power to strengthen the preacher's trembling hands and weak knees and uncertain voice. The act of preaching is like the throwing down of a gauntlet to some who hear, or the stretching out of a strong hand to others, but always, whatever the theme, it is the posing of the ultimate question. And no preacher ought to mount the pulpit steps unless he is prepared to answer it.

2 *The Final Word*

That final Word is 'Yes'. As Paul puts it, 'Jesus . . . was not Yes and No; but in him it is always Yes. For all the promises of God find their Yes in him' (2 Cor. 1:19, 20a). And at this point a book about preaching inevitably becomes preaching for it is through the exposition of such a text the inner dynamics of the sermon are revealed. The human condition is at all points a blend of Yes and No—contradiction, ambiguity, uncertainty. We live with a fundamental dilemma which has us in turmoil whenever we face choices we cannot avoid and yet cannot face. Only God can resolve that dilemma by transcending through the Gospel the Law of Yes and No which has unregenerate man in thrall.

All natural life is under the law of Yes and No. Not Yes alone or No alone. But Yes and No held together in tension. Whatever can be truly said about the world of men is never simple; it is a counterpoint of denials and affirmations. Over the labyrinth of life-directions which we have the freedom to explore, there hang no constant green or constant red lights, but lights which flash green one moment and red the next.

Take human relationships. They stand under this law. All human encounters are of the stop-go variety. A Yes is sounded over our desire to get to know someone better, but at a certain point this Yes will almost certainly shade into No—a shutter comes down to keep us out of some inner sanctum of privacy. Indeed, the depth of a relationship can be measured by the distance one can travel 'into' another person before the Yes becomes muffled and finally clarifies in No. Most dilemmas of relationship arise from this blurred area where Yes appears about to change to No. We say, 'We don't know where we are with X!' And we are afraid to move forward for fear we trespass on forbidden ground.

The classical Yes in everyday life is the one said by a girl to the man who proposes to her. Unless she is remarkably single-minded or suffering from overactive glands and an underactive brain, her Yes has embodied and finally overcome a whole range of No's—hestitations, doubts, uncertainties. And if her judgement proves unsound, one or more of those No's may eventually rise up and choke out the original Yes so that the relationship dies.

Take the search for God. This stands under the law of Yes and No. From the beginning of time, men have tried to fight their way toward heaven. All kinds of promising paths have opened up—a Yes has sounded over the rites of sacrifice, the observances of religious ceremonial, or the way of personal renunciation. And so these spiritual explorers have founded their religions, led new movements, or publicized their teachings, the way to God at long last revealed! But the devotees who have stuck closest to the rules and gone farthest along the road charted by their *gurus* have made the disconcerting discovery that the goal recedes all the while they try to reach it. Yes has given way to a No which effectively bars the way to God; a No which preserves God's infinite distance from man.

That experience of spiritual aridity called by the saints the dark night of the soul has been known to take hold of the religiously self-righteous and sound a blank No that damns the cocky Yes of their previous superficial spiritual exuberance. It is a jarring jolt to those cheerful chappies of any faith who claim to have a matey, back-slapping approach to God and who speak with arrogant certitude about him on the basis of some private intelligence he has whispered in their ear. It took Martin Luther a long time to realize that the Yes which sent him to join the Augustinian Hermits at Erfurt had changed into a No that not all the flagellation and self-denial could cancel out. The way to God was barred.

Take the certainty of death. Here the law of Yes and No is most poignantly demonstrated. Life sounds a resounding Yes to a man—his gifts and potentialities and powers—then just as the world is poised to reap the harvest of achievement, a sudden shocking No drowns out the Yes, and he is taken from us. So we lose a William Temple, a John F. Kennedy, a Martin Luther King; so we lose any man or woman who enriches the world, however slightly. The Yes which we interpret according to our personal philosophy as the smile of fortune, the promptings of destiny, or divinely ordained vocation expires with a sigh leaving a silence pregnant with an ultimate No.

Death's No puts terminus to life's bravest Yes.

There are those who cannot bear the burden of this law of Yes and No. They hate ambiguity and want life to give them a straight answer—Yes or No. So they tear into two pieces that banner flying over life upon which is emblazoned this strange law and nail to their mast whichever half suits them best. Some with brave optimism look for a way of life which seems to offer a Yes without any balancing No. Religiously, they are among Richard Niebuhr's liberals who want to believe in a Christ without the cross, resurrection without the tomb and a kingdom which they may enter without experiencing judgement. Politically, they end up making a god of the state as the fascist does, or of an ideology as the communist does, or of simple goodwill as the humanitarian does. With limitless capacity for self-delusion, they try to deal with life's darker realities the way the Christian Scientist deals with disease—by steadfastly refusing to acknowledge its existence. But sooner or later, their naïveté or arrogance brings them crashing. The No they have struggled to suppress rises to choke the life out of their pathetic Yes.

Others resolve to become life-deniers. Tired of being tantalized by the interplay of Yes and No, they accept the worst and turn it into a philosophy. They abandon all hope and human expectations. For them, the Buddhist *stupa*—the bubble—is the appropriate symbol for a life that is ephemeral and futile. There are Christians with a streak of perverted puritanism in them who say No to life and hope to preserve their virtue in the same way a swimmer tries to keep his clothes dry, by avoiding plunging into the water. And there are thousands of ordinary folk who have been hurt by someone, and having decided that every new affection brings a new affliction, they live behind closed doors, psychological or actual, to avoid human encounter. The result is cynicism, despair, and deadness. You can pretend that there is no Yes at life's heart just as you can pretend that there is no sun at the centre of the solar system, but the result is likely to be the same in both cases—the determined flight from reality that leads to the madhouse.

No clearer possible Yes could have been sounded than over Jesus of Nazareth. His life was one of boundless horizons in healing, teaching, and service. Yet even this sublime Yes was drowned by the ultimate No of Calvary.

And all man's hopes of breaking out of this vicious circle were buried with him in a tomb.

Then on the third day, he rose from the dead. Another Yes had been sounded beyond the Yes and No of natural life. God said Yes to his obedience, Yes to his goodness, Yes to his sense of oneness with the source of all being. And God's Yes is not balanced by any No. It is a final Yes which, coming from *beyond* history, but sounding *within* history, cannot be vitiated or modified. So as Paul puts it—in Jesus it is always Yes, every contingent No has been cancelled out. And those who are alive with his life are also drawn into this realm of a deathless Yes.

In Jesus, Yes has sounded to a knowledge of God not barred by any No. The present theological ferment of our time is only possible because this Yes has sounded. Words like heresy and orthodoxy now have a quaintly old-fashioned ring in many areas of the church. Theology has ceased to be the exclusive purview of the professional expert—Latin theses have given way to paperbacks. The solicitous concern of the clergy to avoid exposing the laity to so-called difficult theological questions is now seen for what it is, a relic of medieval priestly freemasonry, where the justification for the parson's existence at all was the possession of a body of arcane knowledge denied to the ordinary man. This 'not in front of the children!' attitude of some clergy is being swept aside in scorn partly because many lay folk are now better educated than their parson, and also because the advent of the mass media has rendered suspect all ideas which are meant for general consumption but which cannot be communicated directly to the public in an idiom they can understand. And there is a growing feeling in the church that *any* truths about God which are too difficult for the man in the pew to grasp have no value anyway except in those closed circles where professors chase the tails of their academic gowns.

Now because something is happening on such a wide scale, this does not mean that it is necessarily good; but this new freedom to explore God is so consonant with the spirit of Jesus that it must be right. God's Yes to our search for him means that we can start from any point and take any route that is congenial to us. The resurgence of Eastern cults, the growing strength of mystical movements, the ethical involvement in great issues of the day by humanists who choose to make man their road to God—all these and many more explorations into divinity have been made possible by the explosion into life of the resurrection power of Jesus, even though his name is never invoked. Let popes hurl their anathemas and fundamentalists scream damnation, God's endorsement of Jesus as the best human model of the inner connection between truth, love, and joy has opened doors that the combined weights of all the inquisitions and ecclesiastical vested interests can never again force closed.

Supremely, of course, this knowledge of himself to which God says Yes is summarized in Jesus. We cannot know what God is like, but we do know what a God-filled man is like. The new Testament writers, with the two possible exceptions of Romans 9:5 and Hebrews 1:8, never claimed that Jesus was God, but that God was uniquely at work in him to such a degree that when men rejected him, they rejected God. The vast volumes of historical theology with their thousands of pages of discussion of the so-called heresies about the person and work of Jesus show that the study of Jesus is inexhaustible. About this Galilean peasant more books have been written and more words spoken than about anyone else in the history of the world. They are but a fraction of the total response to that Yes God sounded in Jesus. And the exploration will go on until the end of time. No one, no group of school or faculty or church, will ever get to the bottom of Jesus. God would not endorse one whose significance could be exhausted so easily that men were left at a loose end, looking around for other messiahs. This Yes beyond history must encompass the whole of history or it would be subject to the law of Yes and No under which all natural life stands.

In Jesus, Yes has sounded to relationships which are not restricted by any No. That statement could be taken as an endorsement of the permissive society, the new morality, that spirit of our time which the orthodox parody as 'to blazes with the Ten Commandments! Let everyone do what the hell he likes!' But we must risk the wrath of the Pharisees amongst us to stand for a new openness to the demands upon us of our fellow human beings which are governed not by any law or code of ethics, but solely in terms of what love demands. Such an approach to human relationships, far from encouraging self-indulgence and expressing self-will as the legalists claim, demands much greater self-discipline. We cannot hide behind the rules, warping our personalities in fancied obedience to some higher law or doing the right thing with a bad grace because we 'ought to'. God's Yes in Jesus to open human encounter puts the ball squarely in our court and lays upon us the ultimate responsibility for the other's welfare. Hardly a 'Cassanova's Charter', to use in a different context Baroness Summerskills' description of the new divorce bill in Britain!

John Robinson wrote in *Honest to God*: 'Love alone, because, as it were, it has a built-in moral compass enabling it to "home" intuitively upon the deepest need of the other, can allow itself to be directed completely by the situation. It alone can afford to be utterly open to the situation, or rather the person in the situation, uniquely and for his own sake, without losing its direction and conditionality.' Isn't this precisely how Jesus behaved in his determination that compassion for persons must override all laws? So he commended David for eating the sacred bread of the temple; so he broke the sabbath in order to heal. Human hunger and human suffering created their own ethic beyond the stated rules.

Jesus has made possible a quality of relationship in which we may say Yes to the other, unconditionally, guided only by what love requires. And over such relationships No does not sound, for when we must restrain ourselves, we do so not because we have heard the No of the law's prohibition but the Yes of love's requirements.

In Jesus, Yes has sounded to a kind of truth which is not neutralized by error. This truth is not speculation or earthly wisdom. It is not even that healthy contention described by Bertrand Russell: 'In matters of opinion it is a good thing if there is a vigorous discussion between different schools of thought. In the mental world there is everything to be said in favour of a struggle for existence, leading with luck to a survival of the fittest.' This truth which is not balanced by error is the saving truth of the gospel. It is Yes without No because it can be trusted; one may bank one's life upon it. It is free from illusions and distortions.

There is no 'on balance' or 'taking this into account or that' about it. It is truth which is meant to be done. There is that daring verb in John 3:21, 'He who *does* the truth comes to the light.' This obviously means more than doing what seems to be the right thing; that is a course of action. This verse is talking about a way of life—sharing the life of the one over whom God's Yes of truth has sounded. This is truth which is intended to make us free—delivered from every bondage, either to law which may be a pale reflection of the truth or to doctrines which can only point to the truth.

It is truth which short-circuits all the endless checks and balances and qualifications that lie along the road to its discovery. The opposite of this saving truth of the gospel is not the *opinion* of a Greek thought nor the *lie* of moralism but *nothingness*, chaos, a thing of dust and ashes. For the gospel is not a series of propositions or a body of teaching but a cold statement of how all the laws of God find their fulfilment in Jesus; how God has delivered the keys of the kingdom to him and how God has chosen that we be saved or judged by this man. God alone knows why he should do things this way, and he isn't telling. But there is no error in the gospel for the same reason there is no error in a man's red hair or a shower of rain or the wetness of water. It is the way things *are*. And to deny the way things are is not to perpetuate an error but to embrace insanity.

In Jesus, God says Yes to a life beyond death. This ultimate No of mortality cannot be sounded over Jesus because he already has his death behind him. Resurrection life is the realm of a deathless Yes. For those who share in the power of Jesus's resurrection, their deaths too, in all but the biological sense, are behind them. For them, death *is* a biological crisis, but it is not a spiritual one. Between a man's baptism or his conversion and the summation of all things, the judgement, if you like—provided you do not garnish that truth with crude and misleading imagery—there is no interruption of the development and pace of life either at the point of physical dissolution or at any other time.

It is understandable that men should fear death. Would we not equally have been terrified of birth if some obstetrician could have communicated with us in the womb and given us a clinical description of what was about to happen to us, hour by hour? But we must not judge the significance of any occurrence by the extent of our fear of it. The simple affirmation, 'God is love', involves in its endless facets one that gives the lie to the cruciality of death as an ultimate crisis. Love is the drive to unite all that is separated, in time, in place, in condition. It is the lynch-pin of the unity of all creation and, therefore, cannot be fulfilled within the tiny span of existence between a man's birth and death. There are many forms of separation which cannot be overcome in that space of time—so man meets his death, an unfinished creature. But he has been given the gift of love, and that cannot be taken from him. The infinite has been joined to the finite; the work of uniting us to the source of all being has begun, and we know it has begun not because we see heavenly visions or hear heavenly voices but because in practical, down-to-earth situations we can give and receive love. Why else did John write, 'We know we have passed from death to life because we love the brethren'? Paul's statement that *nothing* can separate us from the love of God—'neither life nor death nor things present nor things to come' —is not so much an assurance of some kind of mystical union with God as a simple declaration that we last as long as love lasts, and love lasts as long as God's love lasts— which is presumably a very long time!

Although the New Testament is explicit about the reality of eternal life, it is agnostic about the mechanics of it, so it would not be a good idea to labour this point. It is enough to claim that those who share the resurrection life of Jesus pass into the realm of a deathless Yes which cannot be cancelled out by any No.

Paul goes on to affirm that all the promises of God find their Yes in Jesus. This means two things, I think. The first is that the totality of what God has to say to man has been summed up in Jesus. All the long record of his dealings with men through countless centuries, all the body of teaching and law passed on to, or discovered by, seers and prophets and visionaries of many lands and ages, have been reduced to manageable proportions in Jesus—in just the same way that a mountain of documents and miles of statistics can be compressed into the size of a computer card. If you are not the scholarly, reflective sort of person, you may with a clear conscience walk past all the libraries of religion and spiritual learning and settle for the truth incarnate in the personality of Jesus.

Secondly, if all the promises of God find their Yes in Jesus, this must mean that God undertakes to honour every promise Jesus gave to men. All the promises of God finding their Yes in Jesus means that his breathtaking claims were not the ravings of a madman nor the stabs in the dark of a pious fool. He had authority to offer those promises, and in the experience of Paul and the early church, God had honoured every one of them.

It is, I suppose, the greatest proof of man's dignity and freedom that all the light and power of this realm of the deathless Yes can only be unlocked if he is willing to respond to God's great Yes with his own simple Yes. Then that law of Yes and No under which we all stand in history is not abolished but transcended. But the Yes beyond Yes and No cannot be sounded without our permission. It is the tremendous echo throughout the universe of our own hesitant affirmation.

Thus the Gospel through which we enter into eternal life hangs upon man's response to God's final Word, embodied in Jesus. And the goal of preaching is to evoke from those who have ears to hear that tiny word—Yes! For the last word is neither with God, who has forfeited by his own fiat the right to overrule man's freewill, nor with the preacher who can ransack heaven and earth for new ways of presenting the Gospel, but with the man in the pew. He opens his mouth to speak and the universe holds its breath in suspense as it waits for his response.

EPILOGUE

———

In the spring of 1914 when the world was on the brink of a holocaust, Charles Silvester Horne, then minister of Whitfield's Tabernacle in London and a newly-elected member of Parliament, gave the Lyman-Beecher Lectures on Preaching. His theme was 'The Romance of Preaching' and he died suddenly on the boat back to Britain within weeks of speaking at Yale. He left behind a legacy every preacher should cherish—a single paragraph from a uniformly brilliant series of expositions on the nature of preaching. In one glorious outburst, he put preaching in its true context, enthroned it within the Church and offered encouragement to all of us who so often feel we are voices crying in the wilderness.

Horne spoke as a man of his time and out of a theological tradition now unfashionable. Since his death, the Church has undergone loss of nerve, seen declining congregations and lived through at least two theological revolutions. But these words are true for all time:

Some trades and professions, it is clear, will die out as the kingdom of God comes to its own. But for every voice that carries inspiration to its fellows; for every soul that has some authentic word from the Eternal wherewith to guide and bless mankind there will always be a welcome. No changes of the future can cancel the commission of the preacher. . . . Let every village preacher who climbs into a rude rostrum, to give out a text and preach a sermon to a meagre handful of somewhat stolid hearers, remember to what majestic Fraternity he belongs and what romantic tradition he inherits.

A 'majestic Fraternity' . . . a 'romantic tradition'—such descriptions may sound impossibly idealistic to the average preacher whom I have addressed and whose vocation I share. I comfort myself by remembering that the People of Israel spent forty years in the wilderness, hearing no heavenly voices, seeing no unearthly visions. It was sun, sand and distance—a parable of the week-by-week grind of the preacher who may have little to show for his hours of preparation and the passionate intensity of his words. The world passes by unheeding: his congregation hardly varies in number by more than a dozen or so of the doggedly faithful nucleus of the People of God gathered in that neighbourhood.

Yet he lives always under that paradoxical threat and promise spoken by Jesus—'I will come again and take you to myself, that where I am there you may be also.' The threat is the preacher's awareness that his latest word could be his last—the Living Word may render all spoken words void. Whereas some have heard though most have been deaf to his admonition, when 'all life is alive with his Life', as Paul put it in that luminous phrase which cracked the code of history, the preacher will *know* what his work and words have been worth—a terrifying prospect.

The promise is the assurance that no word spoken in the name of Jesus is a mere beating of the air—it has its place, however modest, in God's scheme of salvation. So at a time when the preacher is prone to self-doubt not only concerning his ability but even about the value of preaching as such, in his anxiety and restlessness he would do well to recall the comment of the Spanish philosopher and writer, Miguel de Unamuno, that God never denies a man peace except to give him glory.

DATE			